Narrative Strategies in Joyce's *Ulysses*

Studies in Modern Literature, No. 96

Other Titles in This Series

No. 76
*Yeats: An Annual of Critical and
Textual Studies, Volume V, 1987*
Richard J. Finneran, ed.

No. 81
*Interweaving Patterns in the
Works of Joseph Conrad*
C. Gail Fraser

No. 87
Stolen Writings: Blake's Milton,
Joyce's Ulysses, *and the
Nature of Influence*
Murray McArthur

No. 93
*The Pictorial in Modernist Fiction
from Stephen Crane to Ernest Hemingway*
Deborah Schnitzer

Narrative Strategies in Joyce's *Ulysses*

by
Dermot Kelly

U·M·I Research
Press

Ann Arbor / London

HOUSTON PUBLIC LIBRARY

Produced and distributed by
UMI Research Press
an imprint of
University Microfilms Inc.
Ann Arbor, Michigan 48106

Library of Congress Cataloging in Publication Data

Kelly, Dermot, 1959-
  Narrative strategies in Joyce's Ulysses / by Dermot Kelly.
    p. cm—(Studies in modern literature ; no. 96)
    Bibliography: p.
    Includes index.
    ISBN 0-8357-1917-0 (alk. paper)
    1. Joyce, James, 1882-1941. Ulysses. 2. Joyce, James, 1882-1941—
Technique.   3. Narration (Rhetoric)   I. Title. II. Series.
PR6019.09U6715   1988
823'.912—dc19   88-22633
                                                                    CIP

British Library CIP data is available.

For My Parents

Contents

Acknowledgments

I wish to express my gratitude to a few people without whose help this book would never have been written. Joseph Ronsley of McGill University first gave me the opportunity to explore the issues that this study grew out of. At University College Dublin I had the privilege of working with Declan Kiberd, whose insightful comments provided a constant source of encouragement and inspiration as I developed the original manuscript. Augustine Martin also gave me invaluable support in Dublin. Finally, I want to thank the staff of the National Library of Ireland for all their help over the years.

Introduction

The subject of this study is the narrative strategies of James Joyce's novel *Ulysses*. Its main focus will be upon the techniques that depart from the realistic method of the first nine episodes. This study is an original contribution to Joyce studies, because it demonstrates that the sequence of styles in these later episodes coheres as a vision of Bloom, Stephen and Molly. The chief assumption underlying this analysis is that it is absurd to separate issues of character and theme in *Ulysses* from the mechanics of style and presentation. The methods of the last nine episodes are designed to illuminate the precise mythic and psychological dimensions of situations that could not have been as faithfully rendered in any other way.

The ultimate objective of this study is to see *Ulysses* whole, in all its infinitely complex diversity, by suggesting ways in which the different narrative techniques follow from one another or even overlap. We should not suppose that *Ulysses* is to be neatly divided into two halves, one realistic, the other parodic or distorted. The methods of "Oxen of the Sun," "Circe" and "Eumaeus" have been formulated to communicate much that is relevant to the plot of the novel. Also, the style of the first nine episodes is full of gaps, warps, omissions and inconsistencies, as I shall show in the opening chapters. No single stance is privileged in the book. The parodies should receive as much attention as the interior monologues; the fantasies or hallucinations are no more extreme than the realism they displace.

The understanding of the styles of *Ulysses* upon which this study is based proceeds from the supposition that the act of writing such a book is in itself heroic, that through it all we marvel at the artist ranging from technique to technique. Again, to say this is not to diminish the importance of the psychological story of Bloom, Stephen and Molly but simply to point out that the telling of it necessitated a foregrounding of the authorial presence that generates the text.[1] From "Wandering Rocks" onward we become increasingly aware of a writer

All citations of *Ulysses* in this book refer to James Joyce, *Ulysses: The Corrected Text,* ed. Hans Walter Gabler with Wolfhard Steppe and Claus Melchior (Harmondsworth: Penguin Books, 1986). Page references are included in parentheses in the text.

scribbling in interruptions and digressions, lyrical reveries and dream images. Harry Levin argued that Joyce uses the styles of "Oxen of the Sun" to reveal himself.[2] By the time we reach "Circe" we have a narrative that is uniquely and exuberantly Joycean. In the chapter on "The Backgrounds of *Ulysses*" in his biography, Richard Ellmann captures the novelistic aspect of this evolution admirably.

> Now Joyce hit upon the more radical device of the undependable narrator with a style adjusted to him. He used this in several episodes of *Ulysses*, for example in *Cyclops*, where the narrator is so obviously hostile to Bloom as to stir up sympathy for him, in *Nausicaa*, where the narrator's gushiness is interrupted and counteracted by Bloom's matter-of-fact reporting, and in *Eumaeus*, where the narrator writes in a style that is constabular. The variety of these devices made T. S. Eliot speak of the "anti-style" of *Ulysses*, but Joyce does not seem to oppose style so much as withdraw it to a deeper level. His ebullient hand shows through its concealments.[3]

It is the author's ebullient hand that lends Bloom Odyssean qualities by turning him into "Some man that wayfaring was" (315) or "an estranged avenger, a wreaker of justice on malefactors, a dark crusader" (598). The styles of the later episodes may sometimes cloud the particulars of characterization in swirls of language, but they also cast mythic silhouettes which result in what Ellmann calls "the ennoblement of the mock-heroic."[4] Parody in *Ulysses* usually entails a recognition of the limitations of language that is nevertheless spirited enough not to be a capitulation to them. Lack of dependability in a narrator allows the author a certain freedom. The intrusive methods only appear to be abandonments of the story of the novel: the comic openness of "Cyclops," the sentimentality of "Nausicaa" and the theatrical conventions of "Circe" all function as frameworks that enable Joyce to shed just the light he desires on each scene.

Parody need not merely belittle or ridicule either its original model or the subject it describes, as Linda Hutcheon has shown in a recent study of the role of parody in modern art forms.[5] Indeed the stylistic imitations in "Oxen of the Sun" are, as Richard Ellmann says, "half-parodic pastiches," because Bloom's reverie over the Bass label (338), to take an example I will look at in chapter 5, could not have been written of so evocatively except in the hypnotic rhythms of De Quincey.[6] Similarly, as I will show in chapter 6, the expressionism of "Circe" is absolutely necessary to dramatize Bloom's secret fears and yearnings. Whereas earlier in the book Joyce occasionally affects a novelistic omniscience to pass on details such as "He liked to read at stool" (55), it would be fatuous to reduce Bloom's masochism to a stroke like, say, "He longed to be humiliated by a manly woman": the grotesquerie of the encounter with Bella/Bello is perfectly right in its way.

Of course the combination of third person narration and interior monologue in the first nine episodes is wonderfully flexible, too, so much so that most of the later extravagances are quietly anticipated. It is not just a question of intricate verbal cross-referencing which could be mapped by computer. That dimension of *Ulysses,* the area maintained by the faculty David Hayman memorably personified as "the arranger,"[7] is an adjunct to the organic stylistic unity of the book. For example, there are verbal correspondences between Bloom's thoughts of the goddesses in the museum and the exchange with the *Photo Bits* nymph in Bella Cohen's,[8] but it is the mutable prose in "Lestrygonians" which hints that the mild-mannered Bloom has been, like Odysseus, a lover of nymphs and goddesses. The hint is triggered by an echo of Tennyson's "Ulysses"[9] as Bloom goes to urinate in Davy Byrne's: "Dribbling a quiet message from his bladder came to go to do not to do there to do. A man and ready he drained his glass to the lees and walked, to men too they gave themselves, manly conscious, lay with men lovers, a youth enjoyed her, to the yard" (145).

This narrator is no more dependable than any of the later voices Ellmann mentions. Bloom's decisive movement is accurately captured, but, as Marilyn French has noted,[10] the language is mocking, especially in the phrases interpolated between the main verb and its object. Here we have a premonition of the spirit that will deflate and enlarge by turns in the sequence of episodes beginning with "Sirens" and "Cyclops." In chapters 1 and 2 I will look at other such instances that suggest the stylistic groundswell of the book.

There is no doubt that Joyce gloried in the styles of *Ulysses,* but at the same time he never engaged in technique for its own sake. Each of the later tableaux, hospital, brothel, cabman's shelter and kitchen, required a different kind of linguistic embroidering and each style had to be carefully nurtured. The letters to Harriet Shaw Weaver testify to the arduousness of the task. At work on "Cyclops" and still recovering from the appalling effort of "Sirens," Joyce protests: "It is impossible for me to write these episodes quickly. The elements needed will fuse only after a prolonged existence together."[11] Again, groggy from "Eumaeus" and drafting "Ithaca" and "Penelope" simultaneously,[12] he complains about the difficulty of "writing a book from eighteen different points of view and in as many styles, all apparently unknown or undiscovered by my fellow tradesmen."[13] The letters to the more supportive Frank Budgen during the same period are full of pride in the technical innovations of each episode, however.[14] In fact *Ulysses* is a triumphant vindication of Ezra Pound's claim that technique is the test of a writer's sincerity.[15] Any attempt to disentangle matters of plot and psychology from the particulars of the verbal surface is misguided.

If the later episodes are boring or opaque in parts it is because Joyce recognizes that any discourse tends to ossify at a certain point. But the imperfections are not devised for pedantic reasons: on the contrary, there is something serendipitous about a book that includes journalistic writing, imitations of mannered essays and bad novels, the script of an extraordinary play, a catechism, and an unpunctuated monologue that reads like a diary or a letter. Actually each improvised discourse exists for a specific purpose, to present a particular impressionistic or expressionistic tableau. There are examples in each episode where the fusion of elements Joyce hoped for has been manifestly achieved. The readings of Joyce's narrative strategies in this study will identify a selection of such passages.

Ulysses really is about "the eternal affirmation of the spirit of man in literature" (544). It is true that nothing much actually happens in the book and that the salient events, such as they are, occur either offstage (Boylan's intrusion) or behind translucent narrative screens (the encounter with Stephen). But it is Joyce's genius that he can secure hundreds of artistic victories from the discouraging shallowness of everyday life. The magisterial styles redeem the terribly banal unhappinesses of the Powers, the Cunninghams,[16] the Dignams and the Blooms. In a sense this transformation of the ordinary, this miraculous ability to bestow a sacred aura on Dublin street names, or to make a man's whole life flash forth as he lingers in a brothel, is the real justification for all the machinations of style and myth. Joyce improvises narrative forms that are often seemingly arbitrary and subliterary, because, as Karen Lawrence argues,[17] these forms record the fugitive emotional reverberations that conventional fiction leaves out. For example, the stylistic duality of "Nausicaa" evokes a feeling of yearning that somehow transcends the rather narrow perimeters occupied by the meager action of the scene. In an acute description of this effect Michael Bell has pointed to exactly the kind of thing we will be looking for in this study. He writes:

> Here the emphasis falls not so much satirically on the character as creatively on the projection of another more elusive and nostalgic emotion for which the sentimental language seems necessary as a kind of base or launching-pad. . . . The naive emotional fantasies of a crippled girl and the loneliness of an older man generate a level of feeling that exists for us archetypally rather than personally. Whether or not we actually think of Nausicaa and Odysseus, the narrative medium so adumbrates the characters' emotions that we cannot get them all back into Gertie and Bloom. Thus, we don't look down on Gertie but accept her synecdochically as the "local habitation," or occasion, for the emotional field Joyce has created in the episode.[18]

Expansiveness of this sort is a fundamental tendency in *Ulysses*. In chapter 3 I will show how Joyce's parodic inflations can attain poetic buoyancy; later, in chapters 7 and 8, I will examine evidence from the homecoming scenes that indicates that certain kinds of unhappiness or longing are best evoked by knowingly excessive indirections. By the time we reach "Eumaeus" and "Ithaca," the distinction between realism and parody has been blurred: sleepily incompetent and clinically skillful, the tired prose and the catechism represent ways for Joyce to escape the burdens imposed by unalloyed forms of either realism or parody. As I will demonstrate in chapter 9, the sublime lyricism of "Penelope" consolidates the gains made by the blurring of this distinction. In the light of such seductively disorienting modulations the muscular solidity of a phrase like "the eternal affirmation of the spirit of man in literature" is slightly oppressive, since the comedy of *Ulysses* arises from a skepticism about narrative and language and a feeling for that which is unknowable in human affairs and relationships. So if *Ulysses* is an "eternal affirmation" it is one made in the face of "the incertitude of the void," to use the words introduced by Stephen in the library and repeated by the Ithacan catechist (170, 572). This phrase captures the sense of existential relativism that is the cumulative effect of all the styles.

The sheer bulk of the later episodes has led to a degree of specialization among commentators. There are invaluable explanatory dissections of "Wandering Rocks" and "Oxen of the Sun" by Clive Hart and James S. Atherton, respectively, in the volume *James Joyce's "Ulysses,"* edited by Hart and David Hayman.[19] Atherton's investigation of the sources of Oxen's imitations is supplemented by Robert Janusko's book on the episode.[20] On the subject of "Eumaeus," John Henry Raleigh has written an excellent monograph-length study, while his book *The Chronicle of Leopold and Molly Bloom* is, among other things, a useful guide to Molly's stream of memories.[21] Of course there are numerous enlightening articles on problematic aspects of the individual episodes, which I will cite in the relevant chapters. In this study I will use the awareness developed by such studies of isolated episodes to work out a chronological analysis of the book that attempts to justify the unique textual contours of each of the later episodes.

Karen Lawrence's book, *The Odyssey of Style in "Ulysses,"* is probably the best analysis to date of the last nine episodes. Lawrence emphasizes the individuality of each episode; her eloquent assessments of the effects of each piece of writing on the reader have had a great influence on the present study. Marilyn French's *The Book as World: James Joyce's "Ulysses"* persuasively ascribes the styles to a mocking narrator whose antics increase our sympathy for Bloom's humanity.[22] French's comments upon the variations of narrative tone are excellent throughout and have been immensely helpful in the preparation of this book. Hopefully my readings will occupy a middle ground between French's often passionately moral view and Lawrence's brilliant textual analysis. I will seek always to show how the styles manage to project the elusive emotions Michael Bell refers to. For instance, in chapter 6 I will look at the tantalizing manner in which the stage directions of "Circe" assume the shape of a clear third-person narration, dispensing supple sentences which, upon inspection, carry traces of the play that will lead to *Finnegans Wake.* One example will suffice for now. Consider this vaudevillian description of Mrs. Dignam: *"Mrs Dignam, widow woman, her snubnose and cheeks flushed with deathtalk, tears and Tunney's tawny sherry, hurries by in her weeds, her bonnet awry, rouging and powdering her cheeks, lips and nose, a pen chivvying her brook of cygnets"* (463).

Here we have the kind of wavering tone that is typical of much of "Circe," "Eumaeus" and "Ithaca." The point of view seems detached, and yet it admits the possibility of sympathy: the comic feeling is mitigated by the vivid details which bear more than a hint of sincerity and even sentiment. Still, both the breezy alliteration ("deathtalk, tears and Tunney's tawny sherry") and the elegant metaphor, lifted from Stephen's description of Shakespeare on the way to the Globe (154–55), suggest distance. Mrs. Dignam is not the "swan of Avon" (155), but the irony of the repetition cuts deeper than that: Joyce's parodic narratives acknowledge the vanity of such elegance without renouncing the pleasure it may afford. There is pity for Mrs. Dignam's common grief, even though we can practically hear the author's purring assent to his own continuing felicity. The tenor of the sentence is indeterminate then, since Joyce has now absolved himself of the obligation to choose between being funny or straight-faced. In its cartoonlike dramatization of the unconscious, "Circe" blows up images that might have been almost subliminal in the interior monologue. The entrance of Mrs. Dignam prepares us for the more powerful apparitions of Mrs. Dedalus and little Rudy. Following hard on the heels of the vision of Boylan possessing Molly and the vision of Shakespeare that will turn into Martin Cunningham, it underscores the desolation and betrayal from which the pervasive humor of this book springs. *Ulysses* commands more sympathy for the domestic troubles of Martin Cunningham and his ilk than for those of Shakespeare in Stephen's convoluted portrayal. In the sentence quoted above we can see a twinkle in the artist's eye as he applies a few gently mocking brushstrokes to an image that is basically pathetic. Finally, it is this quality of stoical heartbreak, colossally expanded in the poignant anticlimax of Bloom's meeting with Stephen and in the sadness of the Blooms' marriage, which the very greatest Joyce scholars, Richard Ellmann and Hugh Kenner,[23] have always directed us to and which furnishes all the elusive emotions the styles reflect.

1

The Scope of the Initial Style

The combination of interior monologue and third-person past tense narration that Joyce called "the initial style" of *Ulysses* is not a monolith of uniformity. Its strength is in its amorphousness. Its vagaries prepare us for disjunctive later chapters like "Cyclops," "Oxen of the Sun" and "Circe."

The monologue and the narration form a mechanism, but as discrete parts they are allowed the freedom of movement to appear in any number of strange combinations. Action in *Ulysses*, even in the early episodes, is never just a matter of character and plot. Many events are purely textual. A single sentence can cause a metamorphosis in the prose.

It seems misguided to complain, as Edmund Wilson did, that the narrative antics of "Cyclops" and "Oxen of the Sun" "spoil the story."[1] It is not as if *Ulysses* is a conventional novel that suddenly starts to meander after a few hundred pages. Any claim that the initial style is entirely consistent must overlook many things. Even those who celebrate the second half of the book tend to discuss the initial style in a reductive manner. For example, in a recent study of the stylistic mutations of the last nine chapters, Karen Lawrence speaks of a "narrative norm" in the first half of the book that "provides stability and continuity" and "a certain security" based on "the sense of the solidity of external reality."[2] This is true enough: the detailed realism of the initial style creates a matrix for the later narrative experimentation, but it also features abrupt shifts and departures from external reality.

Joyce used the phrase "initial style" in a letter to Harriet Shaw Weaver. He was defending the technique of "Sirens," but his statement contains an interesting implication about the act of reading *Ulysses* as a whole: "I understand that you may begin to regard the various styles of the episodes with dismay and prefer the initial style much as the wanderer did who longed for the rock of Ithaca."[3]

The analogy Joyce makes between the reader and Odysseus is not arbitrary.[4] If we accept this, then we can say that the adventures of *Ulysses* arise from the

An earlier version of this chapter appeared in *Dutch Quarterly Review* 17, no. 1 (1987): 1–14.

obstacles the reader has to overcome. In the second half of the book these obstacles have been methodically implemented so that we encounter a new set in each chapter. Contrastingly, the disruptions of the initial style are irregular, only gradually revealing the breadth of its capabilities.

In this chapter I will look at two examples each from the early sections dealing with Stephen and Bloom. These examples demonstrate the elasticity of the initial style, a method of presentation that might otherwise have been plodding. The passages from the Telemachiad help us to outline the peripheries of Stephen's point of view, which underlies so much of the novel. In passages from "Calypso" and "Lotus Eaters" we can begin to discern the dimensions of Bloom's being that will provide the occasion for so many of the outrages of the later chapters.

The great paradox of Stephen's role in the novel is that, although he is obviously gifted, he has serious limitations as a human being. We care for him, partially because, having read the *Portrait* and Ellmann's biography, we know what an autobiographical creation he is, but also because he is a charismatic figure whose problems engage us. His sense of irony pervades *Ulysses* and he himself cannot escape its levelling force. He is not a figure of fun the way Bloom is, however: we are constantly invited to smile at the narration of Bloom's movements, but Stephen's ascendancy over the text allows for no such gentle irony. Instead we watch him bring his razor-sharp perceptions to bear on his own foibles. Eventually, though we admire its literary power, we are appalled by this formidable intelligence and, recoiling, we turn to the simpler virtues of Bloom for solace. So seasoned readers learn to detect Stephen's self-absorption behind one of the narrative peculiarities of "Telemachus," a sculpted description of Mary Dedalus's ghost repeated twice almost word-for-word in the space of five pages. This is *Ulysses* quoting itself and calling attention to its status as a written work, but it is also the narrator, who is virtually Stephen's double at this point, pausing to savor some particularly well-turned phrases. Ambiguities like these remind us that Stephen's vision governs much but not all of *Ulysses*.

The last paragraph of "Proteus" reinforces our sense of the limitations of Stephen's perception. Suddenly the tone changes and a new narrating voice usurps Stephen's sovereignty as the presence meditating upon the world. Ostensibly this break in the surface of the text is introduced to perform the most basic of novelistic tasks, the change of scene, but it foreshadows the jarring shifts of perspective that characterize the episodes between "Wandering Rocks" and "Circe." It also serves to emphasize how Joyce's stylistic devices often speed up the unfolding of events by interrupting the narrative flow.

The first unusual narrative development of "Calypso" involves a combination of omniscient narration and internal monologue, which reverses the process we see at the end of "Proteus." Now instead of moving away the third-person narrative immerses itself in the stream of consciousness. The result is Bloom's humble vision of a girl in the sun which stands in stark contrast to Stephen's elaborate evocations of his mother. In a flash we discover how forlorn Bloom is. At the same time we see that, coupled with Bloom's lively imagination, the initial style can be a very flexible medium.

My fourth example is a single sentence in "Lotus Eaters" in which Bloom projects his sexual desire onto Martha Clifford's letter. The Homeric parallel furnishes a series of flower names which, strategically inserted, turn the letter into an erotic poem. The sentence is an instance of the repetition that is a hallmark of "Scylla and Charybdis" and "Sirens," but its verbal inventiveness surpasses the formalized comedy of those chapters.

Stephen is the merciless ironist who establishes a precedent for all the linguistic attacks the resilient Bloom has to withstand in the course of the book.[5] When the initial style has been specially adapted to suit Stephen then it takes on a distinctly literary quality. In my first two examples of the initial style's protean power I indicate how this same bookishness is employed to subtly undermine the hegemony Stephen enjoys in the Telemachiad. Bloom's sanguine and pragmatic temperament provides him with less impressive but ultimately more dependable resources for the battle to keep his disappointing circumstances from getting the better of him. His emotional vulnerability will be an asset that no amount of irony can ever completely erode. In the passages from "Calypso" and "Lotus Eaters" we see the work of his supple intuitive mind which, despite its limitations, will enable him to survive the onslaught of ridicule that is launched against him in the middle of the book.

Ulysses constantly quotes itself, but we tend to be more aware of this when a phrase from one chapter turns up in another, not when, as in the example we will look at in a moment, the reiteration only appears a few pages after the original utterance. In "Nestor," for example, when Stephen is helping Sargent with his sums, he recalls Mulligan's description of his Hamlet theory in the previous chapter and misquotes it (15, 23). Even more striking is the moment in "Sirens" when, as Bloom eats his lunch of liver and bacon, the third-person narration refers to the words it used in the first paragraph of "Calypso" (45, 221). Because of the ruminative nature of the interior monologue, echoes like the one in "Nestor" occur often while quotations like the one in "Sirens" can be attributed to the parodic strain in the novel. The repetition of Stephen's morbid thoughts in "Telemachus" can be interpreted on both the psychological and the satirical levels. Stephen's sense of irony is far more acute than Bloom's, so it is fitting that the presentation of his consciousness should furnish the occasion for a meeting of such disparate tendencies in the novel.

The young artist's temperament underlies much of the narrative of *Ulysses*. In the repeated vision of his mother's ghost in "Telemachus" we can read the prose of a wordsmith who is doing his best to beautify a traumatic experience. Here are the two almost identical sentences which give us an early indication of Stephen's character and of the character of the book we are reading:

Silently, in a dream she had come to him after her death, her wasted body within its loose brown graveclothes giving off an odour of wax and rosewood, her breath, that had bent upon him, mute, reproachful, a faint odour of wetted ashes. (5)

In a dream, silently, she had come to him, her wasted body within its loose graveclothes giving off an odour of wax and rosewood, her breath bent over him with mute secret words, a faint odour of wetted ashes. (9)

To understand these sentences fully we must treat them as more than the literal reflections of Stephen's mind that they clearly are. They are Joyce's sentences as much as Stephen's and, although there is none of the derision here that there is in the echoed phrasing of "Scylla and Charybdis" or "Sirens," the sentence does seem to be intoned again in admiration. It is as if by reproducing Stephen's introspective gloom so carefully the narrator has worked himself into a self-regarding reverie. It is the Joycean opulence of the sentence, its stylish precision, that tempts the narrator in this way.

Frank O'Connor, discussing the polished quality of Joyce's prose, and comparing it to the verbal arrangements of Pater, remarked, that "reading a story like 'Araby' is less like one's experience of reading than one's experience of glancing through a beautifully illustrated book."[6] Although the creator of Leopold Bloom could hardly be called an aesthete, Stephen could.[7] The studiously repeated sentence above is a sly hint that Stephen should not be too closely identified with Joyce.

There is virtually nothing in the first three chapters to discourage us from thinking that the third-person narrator exists solely as a vehicle for Stephen's perceptions. As we shall see, we are not asked to question this assumption until the last lines of "Proteus." The sentences in "Telemachus" are his attempts to use lyrical language as a kind of iodine for his festering memories. He wants desperately to lay his mother's ghost to rest or at least to behold it without suffering the feelings its approach gives rise to. By making a verbal mosaic out of the apparition he can view it with equanimity as if it were encased in glass. To a certain extent Stephen misrepresents his mother's spirit by trying to convert it into something like one of O'Connor's beautiful illustrations, because it is so obviously a living thing that seeks to pass on a message "with mute secret words." Later Stephen will ask the ghost to tell him "the word known to all men" (474) and it will call for him to repent, once again eluding the mantle he wishes to cloak it in. Repentance is just another one of those big words which will prolong Stephen's unhappiness and prevent him from awaking from the nightmare of history (26, 28).

It hardly needs to be repeated that there is a lot of Joyce in Stephen, but we must bear in mind also that the repeated sentence in "Telemachus" is as representative of *Ulysses* as a whole as it is of Stephen. We find sentences like it far from the domain of the initial style. Consider this stage direction from "Circe," for example, in which Zoe Higgins lures Bloom into Bella Cohen's: *"She leads him towards the steps, drawing him by the odour of her armpits, the vice of her painted eyes, the rustle of her slip in whose sinuous folds lurks the lion reek of all the male brutes that have possessed her"* (409).

The rhythm of this sentence recalls the description of Mary Dedalus's ghost and its meaning evokes certain qualities shared by Stephen and Joyce. Its poetic diction relies on a heightening effect similar to that which is employed in the sentence in "Telemachus." The poetic power of the stage direction would be undermined if our grammatical expectations were fulfilled and the word *and* was inserted where the third comma now sits. In the same way, the description of the ghost would be more ploddingly grammatical and less poetically successful if we were told that its breath was *"giving off* an odour of wetted ashes."

The lyricism of the stage direction is squalid and peculiarly Joycean. The relish with which the smell of Zoe Higgins is described compels us to join Bloom in finding her tantalizing even though her eyeliner associates her with the medieval label of vice. Here we have the values of Stephen's Catholic scheme of things, in which anything sinful must be by its very nature alluring. So a point of view that is not unlike Stephen's can often be inferred even when he is not present. In fact, as we shall see in chapter 6, one precedent for the lubricious descriptions of Zoe Higgins can be found in *Sweets of Sin*. The erotic prose of that novel represents another kind of beautiful illustration, one of the many subliterary alternatives to the initial style that Joyce offers us.

The third-person narrator in "Telemachus" showed signs of narcissism under the spell of Stephen's self-absorption. Again, this sort of duality is not confined to the chapters that center upon Stephen. Here is a sentence from "Wandering Rocks" in which the narrator's irony depends entirely on our ability to gauge what Stephen's reaction to the situation would be. Buck Mulligan is explaining to Haines, over scones in the Dublin Bakery Company, why Stephen will never be a poet. "Buck Mulligan slit a steaming scone in two and plastered butter over its smoking pith" (205).

The language seethes with resentment. We can well imagine the undernourished Stephen penning such a withering indictment of his "wellfed" (5) and insincere crony. In the atmosphere created by the verbs "slit" and "plastered" a simple domestic act becomes a decidedly rapacious business. The rather improbable participle "smoking" introduces an undertone of almost Gothic villainy. In the end we have to concede that Stephen is as much the author of this sentence as he was of the repeated description in "Telemachus." Stephen seems able to make the narrator do his bidding and beautify or vilify whatever troubles him. This power is dramatically exercised in the metamorphic stage directions of "Circe": indeed the imagery of "Wandering Rocks" reappears when the corpse of Stephen's mother is resurrected and Buck Mulligan, *"in particoloured jester's dress of puce and yellow and clown's cap with curling bell,"* gapes at her with *"a smoking buttered split scone in his hand"* (473).

T. S. Eliot told Virginia Woolf that *Ulysses* "showed up the futility of all the English Styles."[8] This statement is not as bleak as it might at first appear. Joyce was not weighed down by an outworn inherited tradition: he was an outsider who could pick and choose whatever devices were expedient at any given point in his struggle to create a twentieth-century Odyssey. So, when the time came to go from Stephen's world to Bloom's, Joyce introduced a tonal alteration as recognizable as any of the stylistic switches in "Oxen of the Sun." Like the transitions in that chapter the change in the narrative direction at the conclusion of "Proteus" is initiated simply with a new paragraph.

We read a series of short paragraphs as Stephen's soliloquy winds down and he prepares to go. Then suddenly, with a formal flourish, the third-person past-tense narrator breaks free of Stephen's consciousness and thus signals the advent of Leopold Bloom: "He turned his face over a shoulder, rere regardant. Moving through the air high spars of a threemaster, her sails brailed up on the crosstrees, homing, upstream, silently moving, a silent ship" (42).

In its way the description of the *Rosevean* at this point comes like the snatches of other scenes that intrude upon the vignettes of "Wandering Rocks." Also, like the epic interruptions that provide an accompaniment to the voice of Thersites at the beginning of "Cyclops," this abrupt adoption of a strangely formal tone serves to remind us that first-person narration (or the variation of it that we get in Stephen's soliloquy) is only one function of the novel's complex narrative machinery. It is a chance for the objective narrator to show that he is autonomous, that he will not always hover around the edges of a character's consciousness. The arrival of the *Rosevean* is a jarring hint of the odyssey that lies ahead for Bloom and for the reader. Even its rhythm is broken by the word "upstream," which Joyce added to the second set of proofs.[9] This interference keeps the sentence from flowing too easily and gives us a small foretaste of the difficulties we will encounter on the book-length homeward journey.

The most significant result of the third-person narrator's move away from Stephen and his interior monologue is that it restores the momentum of the story. The scene is changing and we want to know what is going to happen next. The atmospheric language of the final sentence, with its echoing of present participles, adverb and adjective, draws its energy from the pulse of the ongoing narrative. The mannered diction and the tableau-like effect give us the impression that something is taking its course, that the tale is moving towards some distant resolution. The image of the ship connotes adventure and the archaic participle "rere regardant" evokes a world or romance. Of course these are literary tools that Joyce has taken up in response to a specific occasion. Perhaps Eliot's comment should be modified: Joyce's techniques represent an acknowledgment of the arbitrary nature of any one style.[10] Joyce knew, like Beckett after him, that to tell a story is in some sense to lie. Narrative voice is the necessary illusion which enables writer and reader to sustain the story between them. A fiction writer takes on a voice the way an actor embraces a character. The Telemachiad closes then with a new voice creating a dramatic counterpoint to Stephen's.

Bloom is far more magnanimous than Stephen. His grief does not generate limpid prose; he is more apt to exclaim, "Poor Dignam!" (57) or "Poor papa!" (62). His vocabulary is limited and it is only with an effort that he can think of a word like "dulcimer" (47). As he walks from the pork-butcher's with his breakfast kidney a cloud covers the sun. He is hungry and the gloom makes him want to be near Molly's "ample bedwarmed flesh." This is the cloud that caused Stephen to think of his mother's ghost in terms of no less than three distinct odors, but Bloom's imagination is not as cultivated as this. When the sun comes back out he sees a hazy apparition that is perfectly in keeping with his precarious elation. "Quick warm sunlight came running from Berkeley Road, swiftly, in slim sandals, along the brightening footpath. Runs, she runs to meet me, a girl with gold hair on the wind" (50).

Richard Ellmann notes that Joyce made this image "grandiloquent" so that it would remind us of the golden-sandalled Hermes visiting Calypso in book 5 of *The Odyssey*.[11] It also suits Bloom's state of mind at this point. Boylan's appointment with Molly has not even been confirmed yet and already Bloom has to struggle to maintain any emotional equilibrium. The nebulousness of this brief impressionistic vision is telling: colored as it is by romantic and sexual longing, it is the first sign that all is not as it should be in the Bloom household. A celibate's image of sensual love, it is a false vision, the sort of daydream in which complications are resolved with a melodramatic fanfare. As such it looks forward to the fantasies of "Circe."

There is an undeniable strain of paternal tenderness in the evocation of the girl running from Berkeley Road. Mutations of this image later in the book reveal that Milly is one component of it,[12] but Bloom does not spend a great deal of time thinking about Milly on this day and when he does it is often in relation to her sexual development and particularly with regard to the liaison with Bannon.[13]

However, we really only need to know one fact to understand the emotional sense of Bloom's fleeting vision in the sun, and that is that he and Molly have not made love satisfactorily in more than ten years. This appalling fact, together with Molly's affair with Boylan, is as crucial to Bloom's state of mind today as the memory of Mary Dedalus is to Stephen's. Bloom's muted cry ("Runs, she runs to meet me") is plaintive and in vain, too, as the illusory aura of the present tense in which it is delivered tells us. This is the fictitious tense used for film scripts, stage directions and dream sequences in novels or lyric poems. The sense of loss invoked by Bloom's thoughts of his homeless race and "the grey sunken cunt of the world" (50) is broadened by the vision of the girl. The arrest of sexual intimacy is probably the most numbing form of exile Bloom has to cope with.

The phrases that turn sunlight into "a girl with gold hair" give resonance to Bloom's wish to be near Molly's "ample bedwarmed flesh" (50). Like the sighting of the *Rosevean* this paragraph enlarges the immediate context to anticipate the travels that fill the better part of the book. The image's airy lack of specificity works to its advantage. Our first thought as we read these sentences is that Bloom must have a daughter, but we are also struck by the way the idle homecoming daydream has been made to resemble the visitation of a goddess. The initial style has this mercurial power to open vistas with a few strokes. In fact it might even be argued that the retirement of the initial style closes the doors of unlimited possibility. What was fanciful becomes formulaic and parodic tangents replace whimsical flights. Compared to Bloom's slight but authentic vision of the girl running from Berkeley Road, the ascension "at an angle of fortyfive degrees over Donohoe's in Little Green Street" that closes "Cyclops" is a *deus ex machina*. The implications of the former are much richer. The interruptions in "Cyclops" methodically punctuate the tale of the Thersites figure. Creatures like the girl in the sun appear at much more irregular intervals, but they too are disruptions of a sort. The domain of the initial style is full of dreamlike happenings like these ones in "Lotus Eaters" and "Hades," respectively:

> An incoming train clanked heavily above his head, coach after coach. Barrels bumped in his head: dull porter slopped and churned inside. The bungholes sprang open and a huge dull flood leaked out, flowing together, winding through mudflats all over the level land, a lazy pooling swirl of liquor bearing along wideleaved flowers of its froth. (65)

> Bom! Upset. A coffin bumped out on to the road. Burst open. Paddy Dignam shot out and rolling over stiff in the dust in a brown habit too large for him. (81)

First readers may have to reread these passages to determine what is actually happening, but both of the events described do take place in Bloom's head, one growing from his thoughts of the porter business, the other from talk of a capsized hearse. They exemplify the playfulness of Bloom's mind and gently prepare us for the extravagances of "Cyclops" and "Circe."

In "Telemachus" we saw an instance of repetition in the narrative as a vague intimation of the parodic strain that dominates some of the later chapters. Now we come to a sentence in "Lotus Eaters" which involves repetition but which is more bizarre than anything in "Scylla and Charybdis" or "Sirens," the chapters where repetition is a primary facet of the narrative. The sentence in question arises when Bloom rereads Martha Clifford's letter, having smelt the "almost no smell" of the enclosed flower. "Angry tulips with you darling manflower punish your cactus if you don't please poor forgetmenot how I long violets to dear roses when we soon anemone meet all naughty nightstalk wife Martha's perfume" (64).

It is not the repetition of Martha's words so much as the intrusion of the Homeric parallel in the form of flower names that brings about the sheer craziness of this sentence. Edmund Wilson cited the profusion of flower names in "Lotus Eaters" as evidence to support his charge that Joyce elaborated *Ulysses* too much,[14] but the environment of "Lotus Eaters" is meant to be stupefying and Bloom's sexual arousal has played its part in other distortions too: earlier, for instance, M'Coy's account of how he heard of Dignam's death is all but obscured by Bloom's intense scrutiny of the woman across the street who is about to get onto the carriage. The mixture of interior monologue and fragmented dialogue there was like the absurd juxtaposition of flower names and phrases from Martha's letter in the sentence above. Here Joyce capitalizes on the key motif of the chapter to hilariously dramatize Bloom's use of the letter as an aphrodisiac. The phallic innuendoes of "darling manflower" and the masturbatory "punish your cactus" are obvious. After this, "how I long violets to dear roses" seems to disguise even more outrageous thoughts, the unimaginative images of roses and violets acting as euphemistic screens with a kind of willful inarticulacy that is like cockney rhyming slang or *Finnegans Wake*. Wilson's complaint certainly seems groundless in the face of such ingenuity.

The effect of this sentence is similar but not identical to that of the mocking repetition in "Scylla and Charybdis" and "Sirens." In those chapters the narrative seems to have been read in an echo chamber. The book's tendency to quote itself becomes a mania. The prose reads at times like a jumbled computer printout as materials from the omniscient narration, the dialogue and the interior monologue are reiterated either in corrupt forms or in bizarre new contexts. Among other things, we learn that any utterance can be made laughable if it is mimicked without sufficient regard for its meaning. Here are two characteristic examples, one from "Scylla and Charybdis" and one from "Sirens":

—Do you think it is only a paradox, the quaker librarian was asking. The mocker is never taken seriously when he is most serious.
They talked seriously of mocker's seriousness. (163)

Miss Kennedy sauntered sadly from bright light, twining a loose hair behind an ear. Sauntering sadly, gold no more, she twisted twined a hair. Sadly, she twined in sauntering gold hair behind a curving ear.
—It's them has the fine times, sadly then she said. (212)

These passages differ from the sentence in "Lotus Eaters" because, although they use repetition, they do not add anything new to the phrases they echo. The flower names that erupt among Martha's words have no counterpart in the mocking repetition of "Scylla and Charybdis" or "Sirens." The derision in the later chapters is perpetrated on a treadmill of recapitulation. Limited verbal sets are shuffled for variation, but, because it fails to incorporate the random intrusiveness the flower names represent, the whole process seems mechanical compared to Bloom's transformation of Martha's letter. It is significant that Joyce added the sentence in "Lotus Eaters" to the second set of proofs.[15] The floral rearrangement of the letter is as wild, in its small way, as any of the excesses in the later parts of the book.

We have seen the initial style in a number of different configurations. The presence of each of the two major characters affects the narrative in certain ways. Accordingly the two examples form Stephen's sphere of influence reflect a self-consciousness about the artifice of writing while the passages dealing with Bloom have more of an unrehearsed vitality about them. Bloom's company is liberating after three chapters of Stephen's tortuous thought.

The repeated description of Mary Dedalus is the work of the young artist's "cold steel pen" (6). Later the archaism "rere regardant" introduces a more stodgy bookishness to signal the narrative's disengagement from Stephen's delicate writerly mind. All at once we are outside Stephen and he is just a figure on the shore looking at a ship. In this context the last sentence of "Proteus" is not simply another of Stephen's perceptions: its primary purpose is to arouse our curiosity about the big world beyond his consciousness.

Exploring Bloom's imagination we discover a comic realm where coffins topple off hearses and trainloads of porter flood the land. We find this disorder congenial because it is part of Bloom's bumbling humanity. His condition is as solitary as Stephen's, but he would like nothing better than to amend it. The passages I looked at from "Calypso" and "Lotus Eaters" represent the sort of ruptures of narrative decorum that Bloom's need for human contact causes.

Each of these examples features characteristics that could be ascribed to the whole of *Ulysses*. In "Telemachus" the sound of a sentence can be as interesting as its meaning. The conclusion of "Proteus" demonstrates the arbitrary nature of any narrative technique. So Joyce uses Stephen's world to prepare us for the parodies and distortions of the later chapters. The Homeric parallel brings about metamorphoses as Bloom goes about his business: Hermes appears in a burst of sunlight and a trivial letter takes on the properties of the lotus. From the very beginning of *Ulysses* transformations like these are constantly sweeping us off the rock of Ithaca.

2

The Breakdown of the Initial Style

The comedy of *Ulysses* is not all mean-spirited. In fact the restless search for fresh narrative modes that takes place between "Hades" and "Wandering Rocks" stems from a need to transcend irony and tap the healing power of laughter. Joyce only achieves this transcendence by persistently striking the ironic chord until at last it becomes celebratory in spite of itself. Many readers have listened only to the original cruel fanfare and missed the consoling sound that follows it. It was surely some such hearing defect that led E. M. Forster to call *Ulysses* "a dogged attempt to cover the universe with mud."[1] When Joyce passes beyond mockery, as he does quite regularly in the second half of the book, he sounds a note of rapture. That note can be heard in the climax of Simon Dedalus's version of "M'Appari" in "Sirens" (226–27), in the ascension of "ben Bloom Elijah" in "Cyclops" (282–83), in the orgasmic fireworks of "Nausicaa" (300) and in the vision of Rudy in "Circe" (497). It is also very quietly present in the three sentences devoted to the Elijah throwaway's unimpeded passage down the Liffey in "Wandering Rocks" (186–87, 197, 205). I will conclude this chapter by suggesting how these sentences resonate in their respective contexts.

Although the quest for new styles begins in "Aeolus," I want to look first at the sense of entrapment the narrative's shape instills in "Hades." There, form and content have been so seamlessly joined that it is impossible to determine whether it is Bloom's desolation that necessitates the chapter's impoverished structure or vice versa. I will comment briefly on this strange phenomenon before tackling "Aeolus," which finds Joyce straining against the yoke of the initial style. Temporary relief is furnished by the intrusion of the blatantly alien headlines and catalogues of tram routes on the first page of the episode; they are, after all, mere print and mere facts, but they do serve to detach us from the interior monologue and its trappings that seemed so constricting in the previous chapter. My discussion of "Aeolus" will focus on the ostentatiously mechanical aspects of the narrative that have been designed to make the technique of the first six chapters appear more and more limited.

In "Scylla and Charybdis" we find ourselves back within the confines of the interior monologue. After outlining the problems posed by Stephen's mind and its "bondage" (174), I will move on to "Wandering Rocks" where the interior monologue as a medium is discredited. It remains then for the Elijah throwaway to provide a lasting emblem of Joyce's liberation from his initial style.

"Hades" contains the first signs that the initial style will eventually have to be abandoned. Its shortcomings act as a catalyst for the mutations of "Aeolus." In "Hades" we see Bloom in a social group and discover how alone he actually is. The gap between his interior monologue and the dialogue of his companions is as noticeable as that which separates the two narrators in "Cyclops," the episode that officially marks the dissolution of the initial style. We know Bloom from the inside, whereas our only experience of Simon Dedalus and his friends comes from the talk we overhear. Joyce had to find ways to link these worlds and, among other things, the headlines of "Aeolus"[2] and the musical games of "Sirens" accomplish this by functioning as discourses that are not bound to any one consciousness.

The two conversations that take place out of Bloom's hearing at the funeral (84, 87–88) are only the most obvious indications of the chasm between him and the other mourners. His thoughts are consistently more appealing than the things the others say. When Simon is acrimonious about Stephen, for example, Bloom thinks poignantly of Rudy and Molly (73–74). Our sense of Bloom's worth grows with our awareness of his fractured family and the mordant intelligence behind his taciturnity. This combination of pain and wit (the former adumbrated during the carriage ride, the latter at the cemetery)[3] distinguishes him from the others. They certainly have their share of both, but Bloom's equanimity, his ability to remain solitary without becoming morose, wins our sympathy.[4]

Bloom is a marginal figure among the friends of Stephen's father and yet they receive as much of Joyce's attention as he does. The limited amount of overlap between these two equally vivid spheres may have been what caused early readers of *Ulysses* to praise the interior monologue and criticize the dialogue. Ezra Pound complained that while Bloom was "vital" the dialogue of the other characters was "cryptic" and "incomprehensible save to people who know Dublin." Virginia Woolf called "Hades" "a masterpiece" but still had reservations about its "incoherence."[5]

"Aeolus" dramatizes the provisional status of the initial style.[6] Compared to the earlier chapters, the interior monologues of Stephen and Bloom are only nominally present. Bloom works on the Keyes advertisement and Stephen delivers his parable, but these acts only occupy a fraction of the chapter. Structurally the two protagonists are reduced to monitors through which we view the events in the newspaper office.[7] Bloom's clearheaded observations frame the flippant banter in Crawford's office, reminding us, for instance, that Dan Dawson's speech is aimed at a specific audience (104) and sketching the dissipated appearance of J. J. O'Molloy (103). In the same way Stephen's quotation from Augustine in the midst of the John F. Taylor speech (117) creates an epiphanic moment that illuminates the precise dimensions of Professor MacHugh's moral being.

These counterpoints are part of an exquisitely tuned set of ambiguities which commences with the pervasive atmosphere of mechanization in the chapter's opening pages. Karen Lawrence has said of the headlines that they "surface as marks on a page, as if they were produced mechanically."[8] The same might be said of a good deal of Stephen's interior monologue in "Aeolus." Just as the noise of the presses forces Bloom to slip "his words deftly into the pauses of the clanking" (99) when he is talking to Nannetti, the lively conversation in the *Evening Telegraph* office lowers the pitch of Stephen's thoughts to the level of a code, a series of rapid-fire quotations.[9] These readily identifiable phrases do not deepen our knowledge of Stephen—they merely remind us that he is there. Again, the only really active part Stephen takes in the chapter is the telling of his parable. In an analogous fashion Bloom's thoughts have been programmed to refer repeatedly to wind as soon as he penetrates the domain of Aeolus (102–4). On the basis of these relatively small indications one can imagine how formulaic the initial style might have become if it had been maintained indefinitely.

The deliberately artificial construction of the episode includes more than just the interior monologues of Stephen and Bloom. The mocking echoes that will be a hallmark of "Scylla and Charybdis" and "Sirens" appear in a pronounced manner on a couple of occasions: "And Xenophon looked upon Marathon, Mr. Dedalus said, looking again on the fireplace and to the window, and Marathon looked on the sea" (102). "Lenehan extended his hands in protest.—But my riddle! he said. What opera is like a railway line?—Opera? Mr. O'Madden Burke's sphinx face reriddled" (110).

The repetition of "look" in the first sentence is almost a subliminal touch, like something a sloppy writer might have left in, but the play between "riddle" and "reriddled" in the second instance is obviously contrived. In both cases the narrative appendages have been tailored to reiterate an item from the dialogue in a way that makes one of the simplest fictional conventions seem awkward. The effects here are very similar to the sort of vagaries that are found throughout first "Scylla and Charybdis" and then "Sirens," so it is not surprising that they were among the many features added to "Aeolus" after the *Little Review* publication.[10] These oddities warn us that if the interior monologues disappear so will the clipped realistic narrative that has framed the dialogue. In "Hades" the stage directions used to block out the movements of the characters sometimes seem hackneyed. For example, there are six sentences (five of which open paragraphs) beginning bluntly with the pronoun "All" (72, 73, 74, 84, 86).[11] We can see how close to extinction the initial style has come in just six episodes and how inadequate it is as a vehicle for presenting groups of people in the interlocking and panoramic manner Joyce desired. In any case, "Aeolus" is dense not so much with action as with stagey business.[12] There is much lighting of cigarettes and bustling in and out. Lenehan clowns, Myles Crawford blusters and Professor MacHugh pontificates, but, with the significant exception of Bloom's pursuit of the Keyes renewal, very little happens. Professor MacHugh is sarcastically likening Dan Dawson to Cicero when he murmurs, "The ghost walks" (102), but he may as well be commenting on the insubstantial condition of the shabby genteel company he keeps and the society they represent. Myles Crawford is even more apposite when he declares that they are the fat in the imperial fire (108). These men are creatures of a lost world and they know it. Joyce's narrative tricks ensure that the point is not lost on us either.

It could be argued that the relationship of "Hades" to "Aeolus" is comparable to that of "Scylla and Charybdis" to "Wandering Rocks." "Hades" and "Scylla and Charybdis" outline the formal limitations arising from the exclusive presentation of the minds of Stephen and Bloom. Together these two scenes document the exhaustion of the initial style that the expansiveness of "Aeolus" and "Wandering Rocks" counteracts. In "Hades" the interior monologue seemed to be separated from the dialogue and stage directions by a gulf of indifference. That indifference becomes mockery in "Scylla and Charybdis." Under Stephen's influence, the stage directions mock Lyster, Russell and Best.[13] In his turn, Stephen is mocked by Mulligan.[14] All this fun acquires a malevolent edge from the conflict that racks Stephen as he leads the discussion of *Hamlet.* The tension between what he says and what he thinks is nearly intolerable. The most dramatic exchanges in the chapter occur in the pitched battle between his interior monologue and his spoken discourse. Stephen is too perceptive to overlook the churlishness in his need to portray Shakespeare's family life as a web of treachery, so the most heartless aphorisms he tosses off are undercut by staccato crossfire from his interior monologue. He can hardly claim that a father "is a necessary evil" before his inner voice assails him with the demand, "What the hell are you driving at?" (170). Likewise the quip, "A brother is as easily forgotten as an umbrella" is followed by the unspoken confession, "I am tired of my voice" (173–74). Hugh Kenner is quite right to judge this performance as "a Pyrrhic victory of discourse."[15]

Of course *Ulysses* partially bears out Stephen's claims about the corruption of the family: much of the unhappiness that informs the novel is domestic. In "Wandering Rocks," for example, one has only to think of the stunned grief of young Dignam or the heartbreaking glimpses of the Dedaluses. Still, "Wandering Rocks" makes extensive use of the Elijah throwaway as a sign both of moral order amid material that is ostensibly chaotic and of the exuberance with which the styles of the second half of the book will exalt what they describe as often as they will diminish it. So the thematic concern of Stephen's discourse in the library, the condemnation of the family as a social unit that he issues, is less remarkable than the technical problem that accompanies it, the disintegration of the interior monologue as the central feature of the narrative.

If "Aeolus" shows the restrictions imposed by the increasingly inappropriate initial style, "Wandering Rocks" gives a foretaste of the freedom that will emerge after the initial style's demise. Faced with a series of vignettes that have been snappily edited to include interpolated fragments of one another, one might conclude that the associative principle that governed the interior monologue until now has taken over the whole narrative arrangement. In addition, Joyce makes the interior monologue look like an easy effect to produce by offering us extracts from the thoughts of an assortment of minor figures.[16] Consequently, not only does the interior monologue seem more precarious than ever, but the whole enterprise of character development is cheapened as well. Above all, it is the breadth of this new playfulness, a playfulness that seems to know no bounds, that really dooms the initial style.

Now let us consider the piece of garbage that passes through three sections in "Wandering Rocks," heralding the arrival of a new way of writing that will cut a swath through Joyce's book. Nothing in this crowded episode moves with the beauty of the crumpled skiff Bloom cast upon the waters in "Lestrygonians." It appears three times.

> A skiff, a crumpled throwaway, Elijah is coming, rode lightly down the Liffey, under Loopline bridge, shooting the rapids where water chafed around the bridgepiers, sailing eastward past hulls and anchorchains, between the Customhouse old dock and George's quay. (186–87)

> North wall and sir John Rogerson's quay, with hulls and anchorchains, sailing westward, sailed by a skiff, a crumpled throwaway, rocked on the ferry-wash, Elijah is coming. (197)

> Elijah, skiff, light crumpled throwaway, sailed eastward by flanks of ships and trawlers, amid an archipelago of corks, beyond new Wapping street past Benson's ferry, and by the threemasted schooner *Rosevean* from Bridgewater with bricks. (205)

As three blows to the established narrative technique, these sentences are calculated and resounding. It is a characteristic Joycean strategy to choose something contemptible as the tool that will gradually dislocate the cornerstone. The throwaway is like the "little cloud" or the "still small voice" in the Elijah story: just as, in the Bible, one brings a great rain and the other belongs to the Lord, the throwaway is a tiny message from the comic spirit that will redeem all the depressing human frailty in this novel.[17]

The second of the sentences quoted above is from the section of "Wandering Rocks" about Tom Kernan which is where I will begin my reading of the throwaway's role in the chapter. A number of unprecedented peculiarities are involved in this section. First of all, there is Kernan's observation about the bank manager called Mulligan who noticed his dressy appearance, a brief stroke that is in keeping with the tendency of the narrative in this episode to introduce deceptive namesakes like Russell the lapidary (198) and Bloom the dentist (205). What follows is a subtle hint of the bizarre things that are to come; Kernan says to himself, "Must dress the character for those fellows" (197) and thus echoes Buck Mulligan's statement in "Telemachus" (14). This is a mild example of the textual elasticity that allows Bloom's interior monologue in "Sirens" to include a cluster of words and images from Stephen's interior monologue in "Scylla and Charybdis."[18] Suddenly we realize that everything depends upon the whim of the despotic author who is beginning to fiddle with his book in extraordinary ways.[19]

The sentence about the throwaway quoted here is interpolated in the middle of the Tom Kernan scene. Right after it there is a curious verbal reminiscence of the Biblical Elijah story. The image of dogs licking up Robert Emmet's blood recalls the specific terms of the warning the Lord has Elijah deliver to Ahab after the murder of Naboth.[20] Together with the repetition of Buck Mulligan's words this rather oblique reference suggests something about the complex role the Elijah story plays in "Wandering Rocks." When the throwaway first appears right after Boody Dedalus's line about her father who is "not in heaven" (186) we are inclined to read it as a reminder of the godlessness of the universe.[21] A more positive interpretation insinuates itself, however, when we consider the other scenes that reports of the throwaway interrupt. Aside from the sections featuring Tom Kernan and the Dedalus sisters, the motif is found at the end of the dialogue of Mulligan and Haines in the Dublin Bakery Company (205). Ironic contrasts abound when the three sections are contemplated in juxtaposition. The Dedaluses are nearly starving while Kernan drinks gin with a customer and Mulligan and Haines eat scones and cakes. Mulligan and Haines are as blithely irreligious as the false prophets of Ahab's Israel, yet they fatuously dismiss Stephen's tormented Catholicism. Kernan is interested in Ireland's troubles when they are reassuringly distant, but for the moment he would just as soon salute the lord lieutenant. In this severe moral light almost anything in these scenes might be construed as a reflection of the Elijah story. The soup Maggy Dedalus gets from the nuns could be compared to the miraculous supply of bread the exiled Elijah bestows upon the house of the widow who takes him in.[22] The escape of Lord Edward Fitzgerald from major Sirr, which Kernan thinks of (198), is like Elijah's desperate flight from Jezebel's forces after he has slaughtered the prophets of Baal.[23] Just as the Exodus story lies behind much of the rhetoric of "Aeolus" then, so the Elijah story amplifies the counterpoints of "Wandering Rocks."

The appearances of the Elijah throwaway show how arbitrary the selection of narrative details could be.[24] But, as we can see, the motif brings morality to a seemingly random world. As offhand as these allusions to the wrath of Elijah are, they manage to summon an undertow of justice beneath the episode's bewildering crosscurrents. In his own strange way, Joyce is at once flouting fictional conventions and acknowledging the novelist's obligation to shape his material and even to tell a story. "Wandering Rocks" proves that a good writer can make even the most tenuously connected series of events seem suspenseful. Readers want to believe that a collection of data or a group of scenes is leading to a denouement, so the author only has to hint at a pattern to have his work certified as fiction.

Of course the distorted traces of plot development that we find have been put there to tease us, too, since the pleasure of *Ulysses* comes as much from what Joyce does with language as from what happens to his characters. The throwaway's course corresponds to the passage through the wandering rocks of Jason's Argo;[25] as such it is also emblematic of Joyce's prerogative to do as he pleases with the narrative contraption he has set in motion, a prerogative he will exercise more and more in the episodes that follow this one.

It is always worth remembering what qualities Joyce's first readers perceived. Forster was certainly not alone in his squeamishness, but it is Yeats's phrase that rings truest. At Oxford on March 8, 1922, he wrote of *Ulysses* to Olivia Shakespear: "It has our Irish cruelty and also our kind of strength and the Martello Tower pages are full of beauty. A cruel playful mind like a great soft tiger cat—I hear, as I read, the report of the rebel sergeant in '98: 'O he was a fine fellow, a fine fellow. It was a pleasure to shoot him.' "[26]

Amazingly, Yeats had only read thirty pages or so when he made this observation. It is a frighteningly believable and tantalizingly brief description of the force that animates the peculiarities I have examined in this chapter. Joyce's is a monstrous, roaming genius. The tiger cat that is both "cruel" and "playful," "great" and "soft," seems a fitting image for the mercurial action of the prose I have been studying here.

We see the beast's cruelty first. We need to be persuaded that its playfulness is just as deeply rooted in its nature. The wild freedom so beautifully represented by the voyage of the Elijah skiff is a long time coming. It is hard to believe that such consolation is possible after the gloom of "Hades," the "aching doldrums air" of "Aeolus"[27] and the war of words in "Scylla and Charybdis." The throwaway's escape is a felicitous and absolutely necessary by-product of the ironic treatment the viceregal procession receives. Joyce is demonstrating his new-found autonomy by magisterially belittling the lord lieutenant and glorifying the symbolic scrap of paper.

3

New Narrative Voices in "Sirens" and "Cyclops"

With "Sirens" and "Cyclops" Joyce inaugurates the series of stylistic innovations that will eventually lead to the stage directions of "Circe," the clichés of
"Eumaeus" and the catechism of "Ithaca." In the homecoming episodes, as the
paragraphs swell larger and larger, there is a growing sense of the cheapness
of words and the futility of literary artifice. In "Sirens" we can see the precision
of the initial style giving way to a more arbitrary use of language right before
our eyes. Then third-person narration and interior monologue disappear entirely
to be replaced by a colloquial narrator and parodic interruptions in "Cyclops."
The peculiar verbal tensions of "Sirens" contain suggestions of later narrative
permutations, including those of "Cyclops." Of course the primary tension in
"Sirens" comes from the introduction of a third voice, in the form of mocking,
musical echoes, to offset the components of the initial style. As this voice is implemented the solemn figurative language of the first ten episodes begins to drift
towards a manner that anticipates the deadpan styles of "Eumaeus" and "Ithaca."
For instance, consider how uneasily the most basic narrative materials of metaphor
and information sit amid the repetitive phrasing in these descriptions of the barmaids in the Ormond:

> She poured in a teacup tea, then back in the teapot tea. They cowered under their reef of counter,
> waiting on footstools, crates upturned, waiting for their teas to draw. They pawed their blouses,
> both of black satin, two and nine a yard waiting for their teas to draw, and two and seven. (212)

> They pined in depth of ocean shadow, gold by the beerpull, bronze by maraschino, thoughtful all
> two. Mina Kennedy, 4 Lismore terrace, Drumcondra, with Idolores, a queen, Dolores, silent. (221)

Here we have the episode's delicate balance of lyricism and disinterested
verbal play. Joyce seems to be keeping his own metaphorical power in check.
It is as if the rich metaphors ("reef of counter," "depth of ocean shadow") are
so intoxicating that stray facts like prices and addresses must be planted to
counteract their pull. It is clear that the pieces of information are not so much

indicators of social status as anchors for a drifting text. The randomness of the data is comically highlighted by the awkward insertion of the second rate of payment after the recurring phrase "waiting for their teas to draw" in the first paragraph quoted above. As the language of *Ulysses* becomes more expansive and parodic such information will be divested of much of its empirical currency. A good illustration of this process can be seen in the way Bloom's references to Dockrell's wallpaper change between "Lestrygonians" and "Circe." The earlier reference occurs as part of a poignant reminiscence about Lombard street west: "Snug little room that was with the red wallpaper. Dockrell's, one and ninepence a dozen" (128). In "Circe," accused of molesting Mary Driscoll, Bloom makes a *"long unintelligible speech"* from the dock in which he portrays himself as a lost soul peering in the windows of *"loveful households in Dublin city and urban district"* at *"scenes truly rural of happiness of the better land with Dockrell's wallpaper at one and ninepence a dozen"* (377). The connection with the early days of Bloom's marriage that gave the information its potency in "Lestrygonians" is very nearly lost here. Dislodged from the framework of the interior monologue the emotional and referential clarity of the original detail suffers; but then again Bloom is losing his focus in a haze of guilt and desire as he heads towards Bella Cohen's. We can sense a similar slippage in the recording of Miss Kennedy's address and the prices of the satin: the information's worth is diminished by the apparent arbitrariness of its selection. Ultimately the barmaids' feelings bear the same relationship to the central themes of the episode as Bloom's speech from the dock does to the drama of "Circe": their yearning is part of the general atmosphere in the Ormond while the strange displacement in the summary of the *"unintelligible speech"* serves as a warning that the secrets of Bloom's soul will be revealed in the brothel.

Nowhere is the ambiguous status of fictional information at this point in the book more apparent than in the description of what Boylan on his way to Eccles street would have looked like to a passerby. It is a sentence which might have appeared in the Ithacan catechism. The details are dispensed by a voice that is completely oblivious to their attendant ironies: "A hackney car, number three hundred and twentyfour, driver Barton James of number one Harmony avenue, Donnybrook, on which sat a fare, a young gentleman, stylishly dressed in an indigoblue serge suit made by George Robert Mesias, tailor and cutter, of number five Eden quay, and wearing a straw hat very dressy, bought of John Plasto of number one Great Brunswick street, hatter" (229–30).

There is no indication that the narrator who comes from nowhere to utter this sentence knows that Bloom and Boylan share the same tailor and hatter, even though Bloom and the Ithacan catechist know this (602). Richard Ellmann has characterized the style of "Eumaeus" as "constabular,"[1] and there is definitely something constabular about the way comments like "very dressy" are dutifully noted. At the same time, however, a phrase like "stylishly dressed" anticipates the sort of answers in "Ithaca" that approach the fawning tone of advertising such as the vision of Flowerville "rising . . . upon a gentle eminence with agreeable prospect from balcony" (585). So the description of Boylan here epitomizes the emergent relativity in Joyce's new narrative stances: we know that it proceeds from a limited vantage point, and yet that point is not wholly fixed or personalized but is left tantalizingly indeterminate.[2] The voice just materializes abruptly with the indentation of a new paragraph, like a Cyclopean interruption, a pastiche in "Oxen of the Sun," a hallucination in "Circe" or a response to the Ithacan catechist. The disruption it causes in the text is registered by the words immediately following it, a clipped interrogative and then the episode's musical third voice gloatingly reminding us that the jingling carriage has punctuated the narrative since Boylan left the bar: "Eh? This is the jingle that joggled and jingled."[3] It is clear that the legalistic manner represents the narrator's way of scoffing at Bloom as he composes his lugubrious letter to Martha. Much later on, at the very end of "Ithaca," the exhaustive inventory of all the silk and lace finery Molly has left off will perform a similar function, literally anatomizing what Bloom has missed (600–1). In their different ways the styles of the later episodes, whether they are novelistic ("Oxen of the Sun," "Eumaeus"), dramatic ("Circe"), or legalistic ("Ithaca"), are all violations of the interior monologue's privacy.

Another interesting dramatization of the book's altering narrative currents takes place at the climax of Simon Dedalus's singing of "M'Appari." Unlike the description we have just looked at, which is a bald interpolation, the climax of "M'Appari" is more characteristic of the verbal jumble of "Sirens." We can actually see the felicity of metaphor being overwhelmed by more indiscriminate language. As the song builds to its finale, Bloom, transported by Simon Dedalus's voice, thinks of his first meeting with Molly,[4] and thus the novel's great themes of paternity and betrayal are juxtaposed. Soon the yoking together of these themes will call for larger gestures like those embodied by the forms of "Oxen of the Sun," "Circe" and "Ithaca," but for the moment an explosion of the lapsed grammar that is peculiar to "Sirens" must suffice to evoke Bloom's response to the final note of the song.

> It soared, a bird, it held its flight, a swift pure cry, soar silver orb it leaped serene, speed-ing, sustained, to come, don't spin it out too long long breath he breath long life, soaring high, high resplendent, aflame, crowned, high in the effulgence symbolistic, high, of the etherial bosom, high, of the vast irradiation everywhere all soaring all around about the all, the endlessnessnessness . . . (226–27)

Bloom's mutterings are reduced to flotsam and jetsam in a wave of incoherent hyperbole. The initial style's elegant third-person past-tense narrator can be heard fleetingly in the metaphor that identifies the high note with a bird just before the sentence reverts to the episode's familiar non-grammar ("soar silver orb it leaped serene"). Still, a human voice that could only be Bloom's constitutes a definite undertow. The imperative cry "don't spin it out too long" sounds like the interior monologue.[5] Again, there is a hint of Bloom's ineptitude ("all around about the all") as the sentence stumbles towards ellipsis in the aftermath of all the Latinate words culled from Bloom's memory of Dan Dawson's speech and his thoughts of A. E. and Lizzie Twigg (102, 104, 132, 136).[6] Of course Bloom's mumblings are a tonic amid what would otherwise have been purple prose. That voice will relieve us again and again as Joyce subjects his story to even more extravagant elaborations. For example, after one nearly opaque page in "Oxen of the Sun" it breaks through to reassure Stephen that thunder is "all of the order of a natural phenomenon" (323). At the climax of "M'Appari" the suggestions of Bloom's awkwardness humanize the burst of verbiage, just as the sudden reappearance of a colloquial voice will authenticate the prophetic last sentence of "Cyclops"(283). Nevertheless the combination of the colloquial and the artificial does not seem as amusingly right here as it does at the end of "Cyclops." Like so much else in "Sirens," it seems to be an alliance as uneasy as the balancing act of metaphor and information in the descriptions of the barmaids.

Compared to the brash double-barreled narrative of "Cyclops," the antics of "Sirens" seem like rather small modifications of the initial style. Only in the light of the entire book can we read both episodes as stages in the development of more open and extravagant modes of presentation.[7] In "Cyclops" the lyrical privacy of the initial style is shelved in favor of a more public comedy of beery talk and journalistic writing. Consequently the appearance of a first-person narrator accompanied by parodic interruptions represents a relaxing of the scrupulousness with which the delicate specificity of the morning episodes was maintained. It is customary to regard the interruptions of the barfly's narration as digressions from, or recapitulations of, the action at hand. However, on occasion the interrupting voice takes over from the barfly to relate a piece of business, like Alf Bergan buying a pint (246), or to summarize a speech, like John Wyse Nolan's report to the Citizen on the corporation meeting about the Irish language (266).[8] In "Cyclops" Joyce does not cease the tinkering with the simplest mechanics of storytelling that he began in earnest with all the stagey business of "Aeolus" and that he will raise to a formidable climax with the stage directions of "Circe." By emphasizing the gap between reflection or speech on the one hand and narration on the other, the two-tiered structure of "Cyclops" develops the montage effect we saw when dialogue took place out of Bloom's hearing in "Hades" and "Lestrygonians." In "Wandering Rocks" the careful arrangement of interpolated sentences achieved a comparable effect, suggesting that the associative principle of the interior monologue had been applied to the narrative itself. In "Sirens" the focus shifted freely between the bar, the saloon and the dining room in the Ormond, and even left the hotel altogether first to chart Bloom's progress along the quays and then to monitor Boylan on his way to Eccles street.[9] The transposition of a few phrases from the library scene into the Ormond dining room (166, 230) is only the most startling use of this collage technique. The disjunctiveness of "Cyclops" is not without precedents in the book then.

The first narrative interruption is a bardic announcement of Bloom's approach that is only half-parodic, just as the description of him as an "unconquered hero" (217) at the door of the Ormond was only half in jest. Joe Hynes mentions that Bloom has lent him money:

—Sweat of my brow, says Joe. 'Twas the prudent member gave me the wheeze.
—I saw him before I met you, says I, sloping around by Pill lane and Greek street with his cod's eye counting up all the guts of the fish.
    Who comes through Michan's land, bedight in sable armour? O'Bloom, the son of Rory: it is he. Impervious to fear is Rory's son: he of the prudent soul. (244–45)

The bardic treatment turns Hynes's sarcasm into good-humored irony. Later, when the subject of the upcoming concert tour is broached, a bardic digression about Molly will accomplish a similar feat. Further on down the page from the paragraph about "O'Bloom, the son of Rory" a mock epic stage direction describing the entrance of Alf Bergan shows that the generous spirit of the interruptions is not limited to those featuring Bloom. Alf Bergan's entrance follows the primary narrator's description of his pint of stout:

Ah! Ow! Don't be talking! I was blue mouldy for the want of that pint. Declare to God I could hear it hit the pit of my stomach with a click.
    And lo, as they quaffed their cup of joy, a godlike messenger came swiftly in, radiant as the eye of heaven, a comely youth. (245)

The pseudo-Homeric ring in the diction, the simile and the epithets here signals not only Joyce's affection for this shabby milieu but his awareness of the irony inherent in any attempt to mythologize it. The mock epic style advances the narrative in an overblown manner that contrasts with that of the episode's first-person narrator and sheds a different light on events in the pub. We may remember a comparably wry tone being expressed in the novelistic digression which follows J. J. O'Molloy's portentous lighting of his cigar in the *Evening Telegraph* office:

Messenger took out his matchbox thoughtfully and lit his cigar.
    I have often thought since on looking back over that strange time that it was that small act, trivial in itself, that striking of that match, that determined the whole aftercourse of both our lives. (115)

Here the stylistic object of the mockery is not mannered translations of Homer but conventional fiction. Still, the self-consciousness does resemble that of the style that transforms the pint of Guinness into a "cup of joy" and Alf Bergan into "a godlike messenger." Of course we must not forget that Joyce could very well be poking fun at his own predilection for investing the most banal naturalistic details with the power of myth. After all, the bright light of the morning episodes teems with perfectly serious suggestions of swift-footed immortals and secret messengers. We have only to think of Bloom's vision of the girl in the sun on Eccles street, which serves to remind us of the golden-sandalled Hermes coming to Calypso in book 5 of *The Odyssey*. Then there is the Sandycove milkwoman who, in the poetry of Stephen's thoughts, becomes a Yeatsian personification of Ireland:[10] "A wandering crone, lowly form of an immortal serving her conqueror and her gay betrayer, their common cuckquean, a messenger from the secret morning" (12).

Stephen's acerbity provides Joyce with an opportunity to intimate that the milkwoman may represent Athene visiting Telemachus in book 1 of *The Odyssey*. The figurative language is unravelled with a solemn confidence that seems to have been replaced by facetiousness in the descriptions of O'Molloy lighting his cigar and Alf Bergan entering the pub. The poise of "Telemachus" certainly helps us appreciate just how wobbly the few metaphors in "Sirens" really are as well. In "Cyclops," by dressing figurative language in parodic trappings and according primacy to a colloquial first-person narrator, Joyce seems to have gone further and turned the initial style inside out. Certainly the relationship between the first-person narrator and the parodic interruptions is subtle enough to be considered a real, if comically distended, alternative to the initial style. When Bloom is questioned about the concert tour, the chapter's second voice develops the innuendo about Molly in a way that is far from being unequivocally reductive. Bloom lauds Boylan's organizational skills and the barfly sneers, "That's the bucko that'll organise her." The pungency of this remark is sweetened somewhat by the inflated paragraph that succeeds it. The barfly's rapacious view of sexuality is almost sublimated by a pseudo-bardic interlude in which Molly is presented as a vessel of purity like the bride in the Song of Songs: "Pride of Calpe's rocky mount, the ravenhaired daughter of Tweedy. There grew she to peerless beauty where loquat and almond scent the air. The gardens of Alameda knew her step: the garths of olives knew and bowed. The chaste spouse of Leopold is she: Marion of the bountiful bosoms" (262).

Again, as in the stylized descriptions of Bloom and Bergan, the mockery is not wholly detached.[11] This atmospheric digression catches something of Molly's Mediterranean appeal and even hints, with a wink, at Bloom's devotion to her. The exotic aroma of Gibraltar, which will be so important to "Penelope," is unmistakably present. The lyricism that appears in a muted, parodic form here will be fully developed in Molly's soliloquy. Of course, within the context of "Cyclops," the description of "ben Bloom Elijah" ascending "like a shot off a shovel'' (283) represents the closest thing to a complete abolition of detached mockery.

Interestingly, the second voice of "Cyclops" exercises a degree of autonomy now by following the digression about Molly with a pseudo-Homeric stage direction while the barfly remains silenced:

> And lo, there entered one of the clan of the O'Molloys, a comely hero of white face yet withal somewhat ruddy, his majesty's counsel learned in the law, and with him the prince and heir of the noble line of Lambert.
> —Hello, Ned.
> —Hello, Alf.
> —Hello, Jack.
> —Hello, Joe. (262)

The first-person narrator is bypassed yet again here. We move from the parodic voice to a sequence of curt naturalistic dialogue which confirms the identities of the two new arrivals by revealing their first names.[12] Earlier on, the colloquial narrator eased the transition between the two discourses by informing us right after the mock epic interruption that the "godlike messenger . . . radiant as the eye of heaven" was Alf Bergan. Of course we are given the surnames O'Molloy and Lambert, and the former's "hectic flush" (103), noticed by Bloom in "Aeolus," is deftly touched upon as well.[13] The changing of styles from paragraph to paragraph in "Cyclops" really does foreshadow the patchwork effect we will see in "Oxen of the Sun" when Joyce does away with any notion of a primary narrator. The success of the styles in "Oxen," like that of these parodic flourishes, will be enhanced by our familiarity with the fund of information created by the interior monologues earlier in the book.

There will be two more parodic stage directions before the end of the episode. John Wyse Nolan's statement to the Citizen about the corporation's policy with regard to the Irish language (266) and Lenehan's toast to the downfall of the English (267) are both summarized in mannered interruptions that are allowed to stand without any explanatory recapitulation from the barfly. Still, despite their relative scarcity,[14] the narrative interruptions in "Cyclops" establish a crucial precedent with far-reaching implications for the techniques of the nighttime episodes. In "Circe" narrative stage directions only slightly less stylized than those we have observed in "Cyclops" will weave webs of metaphor as complex as those of the initial style. Indeed, the copious narrative directions in "Circe" occasionally form a second discourse, which provides a kind of accompaniment to the primary action and dialogue the way the parodic interruptions do in "Cyclops." As I shall show in my chapter on "Circe," the aura of Romantic Orientalism that Zoe Higgins exudes will be elaborated in flights of figurative language as sustained as the pseudo-Homeric interludes I have discussed here.

Joyce exploits the malleability of the seemingly impersonal discourses he adopts to tell his story between "Sirens" and "Ithaca." For one thing, the flamboyantly artificial styles allow him the liberty to call Bloom an "unconquered hero" (217) or even "ben Bloom Elijah" (233). The various narrative guises enable him to sketch bolder representations of the ridiculous and sublime aspects of Bloom's character. A certain playfulness was central to the initial style, as we saw in our earlier chapters; now that playful spirit encompasses the selection of stances which will comically advertise their own limitations but which will nevertheless afford generous scope for both irony and poetry.[15]

4

The Gerty MacDowell Style

"Nausicaa" is a paradigmatic illustration of the limits of irony in *Ulysses*. Sandwiched between the colorful anthologies of parodies and pastiches in "Cyclops" and "Oxen of the Sun," it looks disarmingly simple. In fact the portrayal of Gerty MacDowell emphasizes the book's continuing drift away from individualized points of view towards more anonymous public discourses. This is not to say that Gerty is less than fully imagined: she is a typical but believable character. However, at the bottom of her girlish dreams is an ideal of bourgeois domesticity and materialism that is not very different from Bloom's, and so the account of her world shares certain tendencies with the later episodes in the book. There are similarities between the life she envisions as "Mrs Reggy Wylie T. C. D." (288) and Bloom's picture of himself as the owner of Flowerville. For example, the first part of "Nausicaa" and the Ithacan catechism contain fabricated lines from what both narrators refer to as the "fashionable intelligence": "Mrs Gertrude Wylie was wearing a sumptuous confection of grey trimmed with expensive blue fox" (288); "Mr and Mrs Leopold Bloom have left Kingstown for England" (588). And the difference between the furnishings of their imagined residences in only a matter of degree: "They would have a beautifully appointed drawingroom with pictures and engravings . . . and chintz covers for the chairs and that silver toastrack in Clery's summer jumble sales like they have in rich houses" (289).

Gerty's sad longing contrasts with the opulent description of Flowerville, which smooths over economic and emotional considerations because it is more of an advertising fantasy than a fictional daydream. It is clear nevertheless that Bloom's dream of affluence is only an exaggerated version of Gerty's. The language of the genteel salesman is not altogether different from that of the sentimental heroine, as some details of the living room at Flowerville show: "lounge hall fitted with linen wallpresses, fumed oak sectional bookcase containing the Encyclopaedia Britannica and New Century Dictionary . . . comfortable lounge settees and corner fitments, upholstered in ruby plush with good springing and sunk centre" (585–86).

In my analysis of "Ithaca" I will suggest that the manic accumulation of detail in the Flowerville vision avoids the troublesome issue of human companionship, and that the faint pastoral strain in the description compensates for this omission. (Except for the glancing reference to "Mrs Leopold Bloom," Molly is conspicuously absent from Bloom's thoughts of his ideal home.) Thus the pathetic notion of marital bliss that gives Gerty's less flamboyant materialism its focus is really no more illusory than some of Bloom's imaginings; also, they both derive perfectly legitimate consolation from their fantasies.[1]

Although Gerty's discourse is not as varied as, say, the stage directions in "Circe" or the narrative in "Oxen of the Sun," its run-on sentences do admit fragments of other discourses like the advertising voice that is such an ubiquitous presence in *Ulysses*.[2] For example, consider the effect of the phrases about "Catesby's cork lino" in the middle of Gerty's thoughts of her parents. These phrases appear as she reflects upon her father's drunkenness and Paddy Dignam's death.

> And her mother said to him let that be a warning to him for the rest of his days and he couldn't even go to the funeral on account of the gout and she had to go into town to bring him the letters and samples from his office about Catesby's cork lino, artistic, standard designs, fit for a palace, gives tiptop wear and always bright and cheery in the home. (291)

The banal commercial language accentuates the discrepancies between the MacDowell household and the ideal homes represented in advertisements.[3] In this way the linoleum slogans are different from the references to the Litany of Our Lady which frame Gerty's thoughts of her home life and which do, after all, offer comfort to "careworn hearts" (292).[4] Of course Gerty is fluent in the secular discourse of advertising, too: she names the prices of ribbon (287), stockings (295) and knickers (300), and is probably as adept at bargain-hunting as Bloom is. It is just that the juxtaposition of the linoleum slogans and her father's condition creates a singularly acute irony. Indeed it is possible to argue that, since Gerty lacks Bloom's critical eye for advertisements, her religion acts as a catalyst for whatever aesthetic capacity she possesses. Certainly the counterpoint maintained by the episode's Mariolatry is more poetically evocative than that which the linoleum slogans provide.[5]

All this raises the larger question of whether or not the fictional language of the first half of "Nausicaa" is an adequate container for Gerty's being.[6] Such a question is less likely to be posed with regard to later episodes because their styles are so blatantly inadequate. Gerty's discourse is a kind of qualified realism like the narratives of "Eumaeus" and "Ithaca," and yet there are foreshadowings of even the most bizarre stage directions of "Circe" in her modest language. For example, during the hallucinatory trial scene in "Circe" we can see the language of commerce being employed as ironically as it is in the sentence from "Nausicaa" quoted above. Accused of molesting Mary Driscoll, Bloom makes "a bogus statement" from the dock which is as much a tissue of clichés as anything in "Eumaeus." I have already mentioned this *"long unintelligible speech"* (376) in my discussion of the use of fictional information in "Sirens." The speech is summarized in a rambling stage direction that I will look at in detail in my examination of "Circe." The phrases that concern me now arise as the persecuted Bloom describes scenes of domestic harmony he glimpsed while riding the loopline train to nighttown: *"or anon all with fervour reciting the family rosary round the crackling Yulelog while in the boreens and green lanes the colleens with their swains strolled what times the strains of the organtoned melodeon Britanniametalbound with four acting stops and twelvefold bellows, a sacrifice, greatest bargain ever"* (377).

As I will show in my chapter on "Circe," the clichéd description this fragment is taken from actually constitutes a puzzle made up of intricately inappropriate phrases which, when pieced together, suggest the quality of Bloom's alienation. The words quoted above represent, first of all, a hopelessly stereotyped image of Irishness. Then, as the long sentence trails off, an advertising tone creeps in, just as it crept into the description of Gerty's family life. The whole summary of Bloom's speech is full of awkward phrases that adumbrate the cultural confusion of this immigrant's son, but in the reference to the melodeon a "a sacrifice, greatest bargain ever" I detect another kind of confusion, the confusion of religion and commerce that is the hallmark of the evangelist J. Alexander Dowie, who speaks of God as "a corking fine business proposition" (349) and who urges his listeners: "Book through to eternity junction, the nonstop run" (414). In "Nausicaa" Bloom himself considers the analogy when he reflects that both the Mass and advertisements use seductive verbal repetition (309). In a sense Bloom knows more about advertising than he does about Irish Catholicism, and the phrases quoted here subtly indicate as much. So the rather incongruous appearance of advertising slogans in the midst of Gerty's thoughts of her parents is an early example of the sort of strategic indirection Joyce will employ with increasing regularity in the nighttime episodes to articulate painful truths that might be left unexpressed in a more conventional narrative. The extraordinary stage direction reproduces sleepy mumblings that remind us just how lucid Gerty's thoughts of her parents are. Of course the most explicit verbal reminiscence of Gerty's narrative in "Circe" underscores the degradation of her polite idiom; when Kitty Ricketts takes off her hat the stage direction repeats the adjectives that accompanied the same action in "Nausicaa": *"And a prettier, a daintier head of winsome curls was never seen on a whore's shoulders"* (425).[7]

From a purely technical standpoint "Nausicaa" is less sophisticated than either "Cyclops" or "Oxen of the Sun," but, as a transitional stage in Joyce's evolving narrative strategy, the episode's simplicity serves a real purpose. That is, by repeating, in a modified form, procedures that we may have found disorienting in recent episodes like "Wandering Rocks" and "Sirens" Joyce helps us to assimilate his brash alternatives to the initial style. For instance, the limited shifts of focus in the first part of "Nausicaa" can be compared to the rapid cinematic movement between the various sections of the Ormond hotel in "Sirens," or even the snappily edited montages in "Wandering Rocks." "Nausicaa" begins with Cissy Caffrey, Edy Boardman and the children, then moves into the sphere of Gerty's consciousness. The snatches of the church service represent another dimension that only overlaps with Gerty's thoughts to a certain extent. The resulting juxtapositions, especially when Gerty begins to respond to Bloom's gaze, are as artfully executed as the alternations of bar, dining room and saloon in "Sirens." As the suspense mounts Joyce draws the three viewpoints together in a single crowded paragraph:

> Queen of angels, queen of patriarchs, queen of prophets, of all saints, they prayed, queen of the most holy rosary and then Father Conroy handed the thurible to Canon O'Hanlon and he put in the incense and censed the Blessed Sacrament and Cissy Caffrey caught the two twins and she was aching to give them a ringing good clip on the ear but she didn't because she thought he might be watching but she never made a bigger mistake in all her life because Gerty could see without looking that he never took his eyes off of her and then Canon O'Hanlon handed the thurible back to Father Conroy and knelt down looking up at the Blessed Sacrament and the choir began to sing the *Tantum ergo* and she just swung her foot in and out in time as the music rose and fell to the *tantumer gosa cramen tum*. Three and eleven she paid for those stockings in Sparrow's of George's street on the Tuesday, no the Monday before Easter and there wasn't a brack on them and that was what he was looking at, transparent, and not at her insignificant ones that had neither shape nor form (the cheek of her!) because he had eyes in his head to see the difference for himself. (295)

At this juncture the sonorous recitation of the Litany of Our Lady makes the language in which Gerty's thoughts are reported seem impoverished. We saw a similar combination of discourses in "Sirens" when the metaphors describing the barmaids were offset by stark facts like their addresses and the prices of the satin for their blouses (212, 221). As I demonstrated in chapter 3, however, the facts and figures diminish the resonance of the metaphorical "reef of counter" (212) and "depth of ocean shadow" (221). Here it is the other way round: the quotidian world shrinks beside the prayers to the Virgin Mary. The liturgical language develops the tumescent style and the ceremonious movements of Father Conroy and Canon O'Hanlon cast an ironic light upon the girls like that created earlier by the linoleum slogans.[8] It is worth noting that in both cases the discourse that is external to Gerty's customary language, whether it is liturgical or commercial, introduces a more measured syntax into the narrative. The quotations from the Litany and the advertising slogans are reined in with commas, whereas Gerty's thoughts, like Cissy Caffrey's "long gandery strides" (294), often outrun the rules of punctuation.[9] In the paragraph above Gerty becomes a little shrill as she tries at once to assert her superiority to Cissy and arouse Bloom by affecting a refined appreciation of the hymn. The interpolated references to the business on the altar undercut the attempt by reminding us of the absurdity of the sexual encounter that is taking place on the strand.[10] The shuffling of different points of view here is as skillful as the arrangements in "Sirens" that may touch upon as many as four vantage points in the space of half a page.[11]

The position of the Litany of Our Lady in Gerty's half of "Nausicaa" leads me back to one of my central preoccupations of this study: Joyce's use of parodic writing for purposes that are not entirely ironic. Even to refer to the first half of the episode as Gerty's discourse is to sail under a flag of convenience, since the descriptions of the temperance retreat and the other girls with the children cannot always be traced directly to Gerty's consciousness. Nor does the cozy third-person narration tell the whole truth about Gerty; Bloom's interior monologue proves that there could be any number of sides to the story. However, for the sake of expediency, the first part of "Nausicaa" can be called Gerty's discourse, because she is the central focus of the gushing style and most of its excesses can be ascribed to her.[12] At the same time it would be misleading to assume that Joyce is being coldly ironic throughout his portrayal of Gerty MacDowell. There is as much pathos and tenderness as there is irony in "Nausicaa." The evenness of this ratio shows how willing Joyce is to restrict the operations of the ironic mechanism which was so all-encompassing in the Cyclopean parodies. The composition of Gerty's discourse turns the stray note we heard in the paean to the "chaste spouse of Leopold" (262) into a fragile melody. Commentators have suggested that the Gerty MacDowell style grows out of the "Love loves to love love" passage in "Cyclops" (273), but insufficient emphasis has been placed on the subtle modulation of parody such a transposition involves.[13] Perhaps this is because the lyrical element has been woven seamlessly into the parodic style of the episode and we no longer have the awkward hyperbole we saw at the climax of "M'Appari." The achievement of the first part of "Nausicaa" is like that of "Eumaeus": that is, Joyce manages to make language that is settling into banality yield surprising opportunities for poetry and rhetoric. Just five pages from the withering juxtaposition of the temperance retreat and Gerty's stockings there is the wonderful description of the fireworks going off as Gerty shows Bloom her underwear.

> She would fain have cried to him chokingly, held out her snowy slender arms for him to come, to feel his lips laid on her white brow, the cry of a young girl's love, a little strangled cry, wrung from her, that cry that has rung through the ages. And then a rocket sprang and bang shot blind blank and O! then the Roman candle burst and it was like a sigh of O! and everyone cried O! O! in raptures and it gushed out of it a stream of rain gold hair threads and they shed and ah! they were all greeny dewy stars falling with golden, O so lovely, O, soft, sweet, soft! (300)

George Orwell identified a pattern in the writing of *Ulysses* that seems particularly strong here. He said: "Joyce is continually holding himself back from breaking out into a species of verse, and at times he does so, and those are the bits I like.''[14] Although Orwell does not list this passage as one of his favorites, it does feature the two tendencies he pinpoints: the cadences in the first sentence are as feverishly restrained as the moan of yearning they describe while the repeated exclamations in the second mark a sublime release.[15] These two sentences dramatize the process by which the ironic gives way to the celebratory at certain junctures in *Ulysses*. Here the transition involves an ecstatic breaking away from measured diction; grammatically the passage regresses from a style like one of the nineteenth-century pastiches in ''Oxen of the Sun'' to an outpouring like Molly's soliloquy. The hurried conjunctions and exclamation points of the last sentence ease the pressure from the dignified phrasing and punctuation of the first.[16] The dissolution of Gerty's style has begun.

Still, Gerty's discourse is not invalidated. In chapter 5 I will examine a paragraph in Bloom's half of ''Nausicaa'' that closely resembles the style of Gerty's section. It is too easy to say that the movement from yearning to ecstasy in the sentences quoted above represents a progression from the spurious to the authentic and therefore that Bloom's point of view is somehow more sound than Gerty's.[17] The Gerty MacDowell style is no more or less false than any of the other styles in the last nine episodes of the book. The fact that it is at its most powerful just as it explodes with the fireworks and Bloom's ejaculation is in keeping with a general trend in the novel's latter half; the styles are raised to a poetic pitch and then they disappear. We have only to think of Bloom's ascent in the last parody of ''Cyclops,'' the vision of Rudy in ''Circe,'' and the fantastic description of Bloom as an astral wanderer at the end of ''Ithaca'' (598). Again, as I will show in chapter 5, Joyce only really hits his stride as a pasticheur with the splendid imitation of De Quincey (338) that occurs about two-thirds of the way through ''Oxen of the Sun.'' So, even as Gerty's style dissolves, it is vindicated.

The move from yearning to rapture and from literary cadences to staggered diction in those two climactic sentences can be taken as a signal of Bloom's imminent return to the foreground. I suggested that traces of Bloom's interior monologue lent substance to the description of Simon Dedalus's high note in ''M' Appari.'' Now, as the fireworks go off and Bloom ejaculates, the Gerty MacDowell style is amended to include the elliptical poetry of ''rain gold hair threads'' and ''greeny dewy stars'' which, although it cannot be specifically identified with Bloom's language, is more characteristically Joycean in its exuberance than much of the first part of ''Nausicaa.'' It is a playful outburst like the jumble of flower names and words from Martha Clifford's letter in ''Lotus Eaters'' (64). Just as the appearance of the Homeric parallel in the form of flower names altered the initial style in that passage, the sudden record of Bloom's sensations as he reaches orgasm transforms the sentimental language of Gerty's section.[18]

The abrupt change from a mannered to a spontaneous style in these climactic sentences of ''Nausicaa'' prefigures the patchwork of styles that is ''Oxen of the Sun.'' By demonstrating that Gerty's language can be modulated to a pitch that enables it to suggest Bloom's feelings, the two sentences quoted above establish a precedent, not only for the paragraph in Bloom's section that reverts to Gerty's style, but also for passages in "Oxen of the Sun" that bring Stephen and Bloom together in similar ways. For example, the De Quincey pastiche evolves a prose poetry that alternates elegance and ungainliness and, in doing so, continues the practice of mixing the colloquial and the artificially rhetorical that we saw at the climax of "M'Appari." In the process all sorts of motifs are triumphantly recycled: even the Litany of Our Lady makes a ghostly return as the figure of Milly Bloom is emblazoned upon the firmament. Bloom himself is gazing at the label on a bottle of Bass as these verbal pyrotechnics take place, and his reverie is insinuated in much the same way as his ejaculation is at the end of Gerty's section of "Nausicaa." The four episodes concerned with the meeting of Stephen and Bloom feature hypnotically wavering prose set in formats that, however absurd they may sometimes seem, are never entirely discredited. In their own beguilingly modest way, the variations of Gerty MacDowell's discourse anticipate the bolder experiments of "Oxen of the Sun," "Circe," "Eumaeus" and "Ithaca."

"Nausicaa" and "Oxen of the Sun": The Redemption of Parody

In the course of "Nausicaa" and "Oxen of the Sun," Joyce's mocking narrator unseats the initial style and takes over the book. This chapter will begin with a brief look at the mixture of parodic writing and stream-of-consciousness realism in "Nausicaa" and then focus on the parodies and pastiches of "Oxen of the Sun." My only concern in "Nausicaa" will be with one remarkable paragraph in which the teller of Gerty MacDowell's tale gains a foothold on territory occupied by the initial style, and thus establishes a precedent for the narrative of "Oxen" in which the initial style appears only in fragments scattered throughout the imitations of English prose writers. Hints of Bloom's voice give a new depth to the teller of Gerty's tale when the interior monologue is momentarily all but silenced during an elegiac description of Sandymount and Howth in the second part of "Nausicaa" (310). First readers may see this passage, with its sentimental images of the postman, the lamplighter and the newsboy, as a modification of the initial style to suit the episode's twilight mood. However, the beatific vision of Milly Bloom in the climactic De Quincey pastiche in "Oxen," a passage as serene and as tainted with unreality and wish-fulfillment as those about the Elijah skiff and the ascent of "ben Bloom Elijah" in "Wandering Rocks" and "Cyclops," suggests that it is actually the mocking narrator whose ironic intelligence has been modified so that the fragmentation of the initial style can be maintained and exploited. I will conclude this chapter then by demonstrating how the language of Mariolatry and the occult is employed in the vision of Milly to produce a sense of uplifting religiosity. Once again the comic spirit of *Ulysses* soars beyond mockery, as it did in the evocations of the Elijah skiff and Bloom's ascent in "Cyclops." Of course between the elegiac paragraph in "Nausicaa" and the vision of Milly there is the meeting of Stephen and Bloom at the Holles street hospital, the incident that occasions all the parodies and pastiches of "Oxen." In an attempt to reconcile the form and content of the narrative at this point I will consider several passages that dramatize the distance between the protean storyteller of "Oxen" and the psychological realism of the initial style and how, only in the unreal light of such a perspective, could Joyce merge the discourses of Stephen and Bloom.

The text of "Oxen of the Sun" is a web of quotations from, and allusions to, preceding episodes. The passages I will analyze in this chapter highlight this fact, but my aim will not be simply to explore Hanley's *Word Index*. Rather, I intend to suggest some causes and effects of the web Joyce spins in "Oxen." It is too easy to say that the author is refusing to tell a story and has decided to play with words and test the limits of style instead. Like "Aeolus" and "Cyclops," "Oxen" is a chapter that addresses problems of verbal expression only to cast a new light on the human comedy of the novel. Most of "Oxen" is given over to the summary of dialogue in paragraphs of mannered prose. The real dialogue takes place in our minds, however, as we reflect upon the juxtapositions created by the interwoven references to earlier episodes. The overlap between the formerly discrete worlds of Stephen and Bloom becomes visible in this allusive tapestry. In fact, in its own way, the atmosphere of the hospital scene, with all its mad drunken talk, is as weird and magical as that of "Circe." The parodies and pastiches destroy the intimacy of all the earlier episodes that focused upon Stephen or Bloom in isolation. The verbal flux of "Oxen" brings on a nighttime world where the first priority is to show just what it is that connects these two lone men. Joyce is actually inviting us to entertain something very like Yeats's belief that "the borders of our mind are ever shifting, and that many minds can flow into one another,"[1] except that in *Ulysses* the container for these minds is not the poet's "one great memory" but the intelligence of the book itself. There is an endearing humbleness in the Joycean enterprise of bringing together Stephen and Bloom, an acceptance that the projected relationship is doomed to incompleteness. This provisional quality is belied by my fluent metaphors of spinning and weaving, for the allusiveness of "Oxen" is merely a colossal expansion of the collage technique Joyce used to clip Stephen's image of Shakespeare out of the library scene and paste it into "Sirens." The outpourings in the hospital refectory give Joyce more freedom to construct such juxtapositions. So we have Stephen, in a Biblical effusion, railing against "Erin" for committing "fornication" in his sight (322) and very nearly confessing to a knowledge of Molly's infidelity. Later Mulligan describes Haines's arrival at Moore's in a Gothic paragraph (336–37) that ends by cryptically quoting from Bloom's musings in "Hades" and "Nausicaa." The dissolution of mental borders here is playful and inconclusive, a sign of Joyce's unwillingness to let his novel become just a study of aloneness framed with pristine ironic counterpoints. In the end Bloom and Stephen do not share all that much, but their meager communion is still a better thing than any of the other encounters we witness in the book. The technique of "Oxen of the Sun" flouts the laws of fictional plausibility and psychological verisimilitude in order to prepare us for that encounter.

The real climax of "Oxen" comes with the two paragraphs modelled on De Quincey. The final clamoring of Alexander J. Christ Dowie (349) is just another piece of Joycean exuberance beside the majestic pastiche in which the grotesque becomes the divine as Bloom gazes at the label on a bottle of Bass (338). The visions of the east from "Calypso" are resurrected, the enigmas of parallax and metempsychosis are comically neutralized and Milly is transfigured, but the magisterial power of the prose overshadows the relative importance of any of these motifs. We feel that something is taking its course: Bloom's ruminations are being dignified as never before. The first paragraph is full of nightmarish animals and seems heavy with opium fumes while the second is an ethereal dream, redolent of incense. The elegant, mannered prose transports us worlds away from the initial style's fastidious narrator and colloquial interior monologue. Previously the mocking narrator has been an utterly crass alternative to that style, but here he mellows and regains the urbane poise he found momentarily towards the end of "Nausicaa."

Bloom's encounter with Gerty MacDowell is so preposterous it makes his cup of cocoa with Stephen seem momentous and conclusive by comparison. However, the paragraph in which the language of Gerty's section of "Nausicaa" is superimposed upon the initial style in the second part of the chapter does establish a clear precedent for the the De Quincey paragraphs in which Bloom's thoughts are clothed in an equally foreign style.[2] The content of this paragraph, in which the narrator suddenly flies high above the interior monologue, is quite simple. It is a paean to domesticity, springing from Bloom's post-masturbatory nostalgia. At first Bloom's thoughts, with their wry worldliness, deflate the mood of Gerty's tale, but eventually he thinks of his courtship, and the truculence about women that the brief encounter provoked subsides. Then the interior monologue and its accompanying narrator are all but obscured by a paragraph inspired as much by Gerty's consciousness as by Bloom's. That the shift in the point of view is almost imperceptible at first only shows how the paragraph consolidates the mocking narrator's position as a viable alternative to the initial style. The subtle alteration of tone relaxes the uneasy accord between the initial style and the mocking narrator that we saw at the climax of "M'Appari" and prepares us for the sort of high-flown lyricism that will characterize the De Quincey paragraphs. A close reading will show three switches of style before the whimsical conclusion in which Howth is personified as a great sleepy beast.

A last lonely candle wandered up the sky from Mirus bazaar in search of funds for Mercer's hospital and broke, drooping, and shed a cluster of violet but one white stars. They floated, fell: they faded. The shepherd's hour: the hour of folding: hour of tryst. From house to house, giving his everwelcome double knock, went the nine o'clock postman, the glowworm's lamp at his belt gleaming here and there through the laurel hedges. And among the five young trees a hoisted lintstock lit the lamp at Leahy's terrace. By screens of lighted windows, by equal gardens a shrill voice went crying, wailing: *Evening Telegraph, stop press edition! Result of the Gold Cup race!* and from the door of Dignam's house a boy ran out and called. Twittering the bat flew here, flew there. Far out over the sands the coming surf crept, grey. Howth settled for slumber tired of long days, of yumyum rhododendrons (he was old) and felt gladly the night breeze lift, ruffle his fell of ferns. He lay but opened a red eye unsleeping, deep and slowly breathing, slumberous but awake. And far on Kish bank the anchored lightship twinkled, winked at Mr Bloom. (310)

There is a stylistic symbiosis here. The sentences about the postman, the lamplighter and the newsboy cause a swelling of sentiment while the surrounding material bears the marks of the initial style. Ironically, this departure from the interior monologue takes place as Bloom's emotional equilibrium returns: the pages that follow find him thinking warmly of Milly and Molly and even reflecting upon the Citizen in conciliatory terms (310–11). At the same time, the hints of Bloom's discourse here redeem the cheapened feelings of Gerty's world, just as the intrusions of the interior monologue legitimated the extravagance of the mocking narrator at the climax of "M'Appari." Of course the playfulness of the three final sentences unbalances everything by introducing a mocking echo of the Eucharistic seedcake Bloom remembered in "Lestrygonians" (144). The cartoonlike transformation of Howth looks forward to the hallucinations of "Circe" and breaks the sentimental spell of the passage to underline the element of fantasy that is an ingredient in any image of domestic bliss.

The fact that the fluctuations in the tone here are not as abrasive as those in "Oxen" should not prevent us from examining them in detail. Again, the book's mocking voice expands its powers so unobtrusively in this passage that one hardly notices the momentary disappearance of the initial style. The changing contours of the prose at this point anticipate the continuous textual unevenness that distinguishes "Oxen of the Sun." The torrent of parodies and pastiches silences the familiar voices of Stephen and Bloom for most of the chapter and so deprives us of a moral frame of reference and confronts us with the profound unease about language from which all the mocking narrator's antics proceed. Only the personifications of Howth and the winking lightship really approach the metamorphoses of the De Quincey passage, but it is worth studying the paragraph to see how it evolves to this point.

So there are three recognizable changes in the tone before the transformation of Howth. Until then the passage can be analyzed the way the climax of "M'Appari" was analyzed in chapter 3; that is, the utterances of the interior monologue and the narrator of the initial style can be distinguished from those of the mocking narrator who prevails over so much of the novel's second half. The first sentence is like something from "Sirens," a mixture of poetic imagery that would have been maudlin by itself and facts that would have been overly plain by themselves. Then the tone alters for two sentences, representing the two strands of the initial style. The sentences about the postman, the lamplighter and the newsboy are of course a flashback to the cozy feeling of Gerty's section. Then there are two more sentences in the initial style before the metamorphosis of Howth. At the beginning of the paragraph the description of the ejaculating Roman candle as a lonely wanderer calls attention to the Odyssean dimension of Bloom's recent peccadillo. Two of the devices I noted in "Sirens" are then used to authenticate this poetic indulgence. The facts about the bazaar and the hospital establish the wanderer's banal commercial origins and offset the poetry of the sentence the way the prices and addresses undercut the evocative treatment of the barmaids in the Ormond. Then Bloom's voice creeps into the awkward qualification ("but one white") that links the explosion of the candle with his own wasted seed, the effect here being similar to the appearance of pieces of his interior monologue at the climax of "M'Appari." In the Gothic interlude in "Oxen" the parodist will quote directly from Bloom's interior monologue with a disregard for plausibility that will shake the realistic foundations of the novel, but after the strangeness of the first sentence in the paragraph above Joyce lapses into the initial style in order to quell our fears that the relative tameness of his technique in "Nausicaa" was about to be abandoned in favor of a more adventurous format.

The next two sentences only amount to fifteen words in all, one describing the fading of the stars with three clipped verbs, the other meditating upon the connotations of the hour in phrases without verbs. These can be attributed to the third-person past-tense narrator of the initial style and Bloom's interior monologue, respectively. The deliberate precision of that narrator can be discerned in the images of the bat that "flew here, flew there" and of "the coming surf," but it is the slacker narrator of Gerty's section who shrouds the postman, the lamplighter and the newsboy in a lyrical aura of domesticity while reawakening the sense of suburban panorama from "Wandering Rocks" with the indefinite articles of "a hoisted lintstock" and "a shrill voice." The description of Howth settling for slumber "tired of long days" sounds like a return to Gerty's discourse, but a more jarring irony informs the reference to "yumyum rhododendrons" and the parenthetical admission that Bloom is old could be piteous or mocking, just as the lightship's wink could be a taunt or a gesture of encouragement. The comic yoking together of the seedcake and the rhododendrons suggests the spirited way the narrator of "Oxen" will synthesize various motifs; for instance, the De Quincey pastiche will bring together two words, *parallax* and *metempsychosis,* that originally entered Bloom's mind at a space of about a hundred pages from one another in the episodes of "Lestrygonians" and "Calypso." They surface rather haphazardly and offset the opulent prose the way the reference to "yumyum rhododendrons" surfaces here just when we think the teller of Gerty's tale is about to fashion another straightforward, heart-warming sentence. Finally, the vigilant, red-eyed Leviathan of the second-last sentence foreshadows the oppressive beasts of the De Quincey reverie and, by extension, all the hallucinatory transformations of "Oxen."

Although the two parts of "Nausicaa" are as discrete as any two imitations in "Oxen," the stylistic shifts in this paragraph between the different tones associated with Gerty and Bloom are achieved more smoothly than many such transitions in the following episode. Since my analysis may have reduced the development of the paragraph to a series of crude signals, I should mention in passing that Joyce took considerable pains to arrive at the version we have. The textual evolution of the paragraph is fascinating. Many of the features noted were added in Joyce's revisions, which practically doubled the length of the passage. The references to the hospital and the bazaar were added in the margin of the manuscript, as was the sentence about the newsboy. After this, intricate adjustments were made to produce the sculpted prose of the final version. The bat was originally described as flying "here and there" and the newsboy as "crying plaintively"; the streamlining of these details seems to have led to the addition of the sentence about the postman and Bloom's meditation upon the connotations of the hour to typescripts and proofs respectively. So gradually a balance was achieved between the verbal exactness of the initial style and the leisurely manner of Gerty's section.[3]

The symbiotic accord here between Bloom's consciousness and the book's emergent spirit of mockery, as it is embodied in the first part of "Nausicaa," is happier than that which was achieved at the climax of "M'Appari." Simon Dedalus's high note found Bloom's soul in turmoil and the utterances of the interior monologue at that point in "Sirens" were agitated, but it is a more relaxed figure altogether whose soporific presence elicits some relatively sincere work from the narrator, who was generally disinterested and ironic in his portrayal of Gerty MacDowell.[4] Now I come to "Oxen of the Sun," the mocking narrator's most ambitious undertaking and the closest thing to a solo flight he manages. The clearest precedent for the motley sequence of parodies and pastiches lies in the interruptions of "Cyclops" where the mocking narrator leaps boldly from one style to another. And yet, in a certain sense, "Oxen" is a double narrative like "Sirens," even though it lacks the emotional intimacy that the gibes of the mocking narrator were designed to combat in that chapter; the structure of "Oxen" is dichotomized insofar as the residual, fragmented presence of the initial style is substantial enough to merit recognition as the theme upon which the episode's parodic variations are played. Like "Sirens," "Oxen" is a text in which the tone may be altered by a phrase, or even a word, strategically placed. As he composes his imitations of historic English prose styles, the mocking narrator includes shards of Joyce's initial style in juxtapositions that cause us to ask what the relationship of Stephen and Bloom will signify. "Oxen" is like a fiction-writing workshop in which the new narrator of the book's second half tries out various styles and toys with the words and images of the initial style. The effect of this play is to alert us to the number of possible configurations there are for the intersecting themes of *Ulysses*. The spectacle of "Oxen" demonstrates that in this novel the process of echoing words, images and motifs is potentially endless,[5] so the technique of the episode represents an important step towards "Circe" and "Ithaca," where Stephen and Bloom are distorted and magnified until they become like figures in a myth, embodying characteristics that are universal. Critics rightly point out that the parodies expose the limitations of style,[6] but the fact that they also celebrate the labyrinthine complexity of *Ulysses* as a verbal and poetic artifact should not be overlooked either. At the same time, although the intimacy of earlier episodes must be forsaken so that a theater may be created in which the peculiar dilemmas of Stephen and Bloom can resonate in counterpoint, the tone is not uniformly droll or ironic and impersonal. For instance, Bloom's fatherly solicitude at the sight of his friend's drunk son is poignantly rendered in imitations of Malory and Pater (320, 344) that evoke some of the tenderest memories he and Molly share.[7] These passages chillingly underline the solitude in which the three central characters live, solitude that is only temporarily and partially broken in "Eumaeus" and "Ithaca." So all Joyce's literary power is expended to dramatize relationships between characters who are ultimately alone with their thoughts. Also, by far the greater portion of these relationships exists solely in our minds as we read, although even an ideal Joycean insomniac cannot possibly see the book whole, its cross-referencing is so kaleidoscopic.

The symbiosis of mocking narrator and initial style that we saw at the height of Simon Dedalus's song and in the afterglow of the encounter with Gerty Mac-Dowell will not suffice to create all the arresting juxtapositions that the meeting of Stephen and Bloom suggests. For this task Joyce must have the freedom to range over a selection of styles. Night falls and the mocking narrator preys upon the initial style, turning the clear thoughts of the day into morbid rhetoric. Stephen's Biblical castigation of Erin for her treachery is a case in point. It is ostentatiously rich in implications, evoking not only Boylan and Molly but Bannon and Milly, Gertrude and Claudius, Ann Hathaway and Shakespeare's brothers and, of course, Penelope's suitors. The sense here that acts of betrayal underlie all human affairs contrasts markedly with the invocation of the sacred ground of the Blooms' courtship in the paragraph examined in "Nausicaa." There the narrator of Gerty's section hovered enchantingly close to the precision of the initial style. We hardly noticed the creeping sentiment in Bloom's view of the seaside at twilight, and the chimerical representation of Howth was our only warning that we were about to be tumbled into the stylistic whirlpool of "Oxen." "Oxen" jolts us from one mode to another at a breakneck pace, turning items from 1904 Dublin into archetypal motifs with disarming swiftness. The episode is rife with talk and Joyce veils the effusions of his carousers in so many different idioms that, as J. S. Atherton has demonstrated, it is often impossible to tell where the borders between the imitations lie.[8] Consider Stephen's Biblical apostrophe, for example: appearing at the end of a section based on Elizabethan prose and just before the parody of Sir Thomas Browne, it refers, implausibly, to the liaisons with Boylan and Bannon, as if Stephen's drunken sarcasm has somehow made him privy to all the secrets of the Bloom household.

Remember, Erin, thy generations and thy days of old, how thou settedst little by me and by my word and broughtest in a stranger to my gates to commit fornication in my sight and to wax fat and kick like Jeshurum. Therefore hast thou sinned against the light and hast made

me, thy lord, to be the slave of servants. Return, return, Clan Milly: forget me not, O Mile-
sian. Why hast thou done this abomination before me that thou didst spurn me for a merchant
of jalaps and didst deny me to the Roman and the Indian of dark speech with whom thy daughters
did lie luxuriously? Look forth now, my people, upon the land of behest, even from Horeb
and from Nebo and from Pisgah and from the Horns of Hatten unto a land flowing with milk
and money. But thou hast suckled me with a bitter milk: my moon and my sun thou hast quenched
forever. And thou hast left me alone for ever in the dark ways of my bitterness: and with a
kiss of ashes hast thou kissed my mouth. (322)

Stephen might have said something like this, but he would not have guessed
what Molly and Milly are doing. Nor is this another teasing parallel like the assertion that Shakespeare was a cuckold. It is clear, rather, that the author is tamper-
ing with the parodic summaries of his characters' speeches in order to draw our
attention to the treasury of words and images he has accumulated over the last
three hundred pages, a storehouse that can be plundered at will. There is a precious
but affecting forlornness here, however, that not even the puns about "Clan Milly"
and the "land flowing with milk and money" or the pomposity of the Biblical
names and diction can completely obscure.

Although the tone is inconsistent because the passage is overloaded with poetic
connotations, this associative abundance is still rewarding. Stephen seems to be
likening himself to the betrayed Christ,[9] the resentful Hamlet and perhaps even
Milton's defeated Satan.[10] There are also reminiscences of the ghost of Mrs.
Dedalus breathing "a faint odour of wetted ashes" (5, 9), of Hamlet's vision
of Gertrude with Claudius "In the rank sweat of an unseamèd bed, / Stewed in
corruption, honeying and making love / Over the nasty sty,"[11] and of Bloom's
daydream of the east in which a mother "calls her children home in their dark
language" (47), but the most meaningful correspondence is also the least obvious.
The overripe scent here recalls the dreams of the east Stephen and Bloom both
had the night before. The archaic severity of the term *fornication* and the disgust
with the "luxuriously" lying daughters that verges on jealousy suggest that Stephen
feels humiliated in his drunkenness, perhaps realizing that the revelatory promise
of his dream of Haroun al Raschid from the *Arabian Nights* (39, 179) will not
be fulfilled, at least not today. Bloom has had an oriental dream, too, we discover
in "Nausicaa" when he thinks of the condom in his wallet, a dream of ritual
seduction in which Molly appears in Turkish slippers and breeches (303, 311–12),
as she will in "Circe" (359) and "Penelope" (641). Both dreams involve arrival
and entry into an aromatic sensual world. So the uneven tone and unnatural
language of the Biblical apostrophe allow Joyce to blur the unconscious lives of
Stephen and Bloom.[12] Indeed, far from being a smugly ironic capitulation to the
inadequacies of language, the collage of styles in "Oxen" is a valiant attempt
to overcome them. The appearance of Stephen's image from the library scene
in "Sirens" prompted us to compare the cuckolding of Bloom to that of
Shakespeare. Likewise, the tone of Gerty's story was revived to describe Bloom's

impressions of Sandymount and Howth so that we might reflect upon the kind of feelings the adolescent and the middle-aged man have in common. These juxtapositions are more immediately compelling than the correspondence between the dreams of Joyce's heroes suggested by the Biblical speech, but this rather hazy correspondence is important because it initiates the comparative process that will come to fruition in the De Quincey pastiche, when the discourses of Stephen and Bloom are symbiotically mingled. The string of distorted imitations in "Oxen" is only as uneven as the area of overlap between those two worlds.

The tenuous linking of the remote experiences of Stephen and Bloom in the archetypal pattern furnished by the oblique Biblical language will be strengthened in the hallucinatory De Quincey paragraphs. Meanwhile Mulligan's Gothic account of Haines's arrival at Moore's plummets us even further from the cozy domesticity we saw in "Nausicaa" and sets the tone for the pregnant description of Bloom's reverie over the Bass label. One of the reasons the elegiac paragraph in "Nausicaa" rings true is that it touches upon the great glory of the novel, the love of Bloom and Molly; of course the hint of danger in the personification of Howth as a watchful beast reminds us of the crucible their marriage is now passing through. Behind the righteous indignation of the Biblical apostrophe lies Stephen's suspicion that the rupture of such bonds is part of the natural order of things. The Gothic interlude describes a world of treachery, too, but its stylized atmosphere is not as daunting. The language of a recognizable fictional genre is less foreboding than that of the Bible, evoking as it does a neutralized domain of commercial entertainment. The Gothic parody mocks the idea of narrative closure by imitating a piece of formulaic writing in which loose ends are tied up in an entirely arbitrary fashion. This cheerful lack of finality gives Joyce the opportunity to develop the kinship between Stephen and Bloom suggested by the former's prophetic lament. The blurring of their unconscious lives in that passage might have been mere coincidence, but the quotations from Bloom's interior monologue in the Gothic spoof underline the superstition with which Joyce viewed such luck.

As I will demonstrate, the actual phrases that are resurrected are not terribly significant in themselves. The important thing about these quotations of Bloom is that they dramatize the fluidity of the text. One of the clearest examples of this fluidity occurs towards the end of "Circe" when Stephen's mother beseeches him to repent and he cries, "Raw head and bloody bones" (474), thus reproducing a phrase from Bloom's memories of the cattlemarket in "Lestrygonians" (140). In fact the phrase was belatedly planted in Bloom's mind as an addition to the first set of proofs for the episode.[13] It is a small masterstroke, however, linking Bloom's horror at the thought of bloodshed to Stephen's flight from a strangling ancestral religion. The Gothic paragraph was itself added to an early draft of "Oxen of the Sun." It amplifies the narrative treatment of Mulligan and Haines in "Wandering Rocks" that played upon an almost Gothic sense of evil.

But Malachias' tale began to freeze them with horror. He conjured up the scene before them. The secret panel beside the chimney slid back and in the recess appeared . . . Haines! Which of us did not feel his flesh creep? He had a portfolio full of Celtic literature in one hand, in the other a phial marked *Poison*. Surprise, horror, loathing were depicted on all faces while he eyed them with a ghastly grin. I anticipated some such reception, he began with an eldritch laugh, for which, it seems, history is to blame. (336)

The tone is consistently melodramatic here, the only incongruity being Haines's repetition of the excuse he made in "Telemachus" for England's domination of Ireland (17), a familiar phrase that breaks the spell of the imitation the way the puns about "Clan Milly" and the "land flowing with milk and money" undercut the Biblical solemnity of Stephen's speech. No attempt is made to present a balanced account of the scene. Instead the intention seems to be to work in as many disparate motifs as possible even if it means setting aside all notions of fictional plausibility. One incongruity leads to another as the passage develops. Just as Stephen does not know Milly, Haines would not have confessed to the murder of Samuel Childs as he does in the middle of the Gothic paragraph (336), especially since the victim's name was Thomas.

The question of plausibility is hardly relevant beside the web of references to earlier episodes that the passage spins: in fact there is only one line that could reasonably be attributed to Haines, "Meet me at Westland row station at ten past eleven" (337), and it appears two-thirds of the way through the paragraph. By this time the verbal overflow has commenced with Haines bursting into Hiberno-English dialect ("Tare and ages, what way would I be resting at all . . . and I tramping Dublin this while back with my share of songs and himself after me the like of a soulth or a bulawurrus?"), attempting to construct the sort of aphorism that Stephen might have coined in a dull moment ("My hell, and Ireland's is in this life") and raving about his dream of a black panther (336–37). So, like every other model Joyce uses in "Oxen," the Gothic novel is exploited to increase the verbal riches of *Ulysses*. In fact, by replaying lines from earlier episodes this passage sets in motion so many trains of association that it is possible to see it as an embryonic manifestation of the dense technique of *Finnegans Wake*. After the single plausible line from Haines the paragraph winds down, parodying the tableau at the end of a thriller.

He was gone! Tears gushed from the eyes of the dissipated host. The seer raised his hand to heaven, murmuring: The vendetta of Mananaan! The sage repeated *Lex talionis*. The sentimentalist is he who would enjoy without incurring the immense debtorship for a thing done. Malachias, overcome by emotion, ceased. The mystery was unveiled. Haines was the third brother. His real name was Childs. The black panther was himself the ghost of his own father. He drank drugs to obliterate. For this relief much thanks. The lonely house by the graveyard is uninhabited. No soul will live there. The spider pitches her web in the solitude. The nocturnal rat peers from his hole. A curse is on it. It is haunted. Murderer's ground. (337)

There is a growing sense of exhaustion here. The concluding lines might be the idle scribblings of a novelist whose strength is spent and we may suspect that it is Joyce who is spinning his web in solitude. The imitation of bad fiction is as dismayingly authentic as it is in "Eumaeus" and, although the quotations of Bloom substantiate the kinship between the two heroes that was implied in the Biblical passage, the connection still seems more coincidental than organic. *Ulysses* is a kind of mystery story in which the reader is the sleuth, however, and the clues to the secret bond between Stephen and Bloom are beginning to add up as Joyce gradually prepares us for the miraculous symbiosis of the De Quincey passage. Hugh Kenner identifies "the dissipated host," "the seer" and "the sage" as Moore, Russell and Eglinton.[14] Somewhere behind all the ridiculous exaggerations we can imagine Mulligan describing the reaction to Haines's arrival. The attribution of all this to Mulligan is a shrewd dislocating tactic, for the scattered references to Stephen's telegram (164), Mulligan's own joking summary of the Hamlet theory (15) and the conjecture about Shakespeare's brothers (171–74) are as random as the quotations from Bloom's interior monologue that follow and the whole hodgepodge suits Mulligan's jesting style. As the echoes of "Scylla and Charybdis" die down, the writing is reduced to a series of terse sentences including the line from the first scene of *Hamlet* ("For this relief much thanks") that occurs to Bloom as Gerty passes out of sight (305) and culminating in the truncated phrase ("Murderer's ground") from his reflections on the Childs house in Glasnevin (82). We may contrast Bloom's good sense and ability to live for the moment with Stephen's cleverness and studied gloom, but the juxtaposition proves nothing conclusive about their relationship. It is interesting, too, that these last six brief sentences only emerged as afterthoughts in the typescript of the chapter.[15]

The De Quincey paragraphs stand between the imitations of Charles Lamb and Landor. The reminiscences of Bloom's youth in the Lamb paragraph establish the mood of introspection for the De Quincey pastiche. Then the Landor imitation opens with Stephen bragging about his ability to bring the phantoms of his past back to life through the metempsychosis of art and closes with Stephen and Mulligan posing as theosophical interpreters of Bloom's reverie. Essentially the two paragraphs in the style of De Quincey resurrect Bloom's visions of the east from "Calypso" and decorate them in ornate language that removes them from his customary idiom. In the hypnotic prose I see an alignment of the separate consciousnesses of Stephen and Bloom that I find more satisfying than the attempts to connect them in either the Biblical speech or the Gothic parody. Again, the apocalyptic visions are framed by Bloom's meditation on his sonlessness at the end of the Lamb paragraph and Lynch's reproach to Stephen for his artistic barrenness at the beginning of the Landor paragraph, so we are reminded what each of them could gain from their liaison.

In the De Quincey imitation itself there are references to parallax, metempsychosis, Dlugacz's Agendath Netaim advertisement, "M'Appari," Boylan's song about the seaside girls and, of course, Milly Bloom. Bloom's entire odyssey is included by implication. He imagines Palestine so vividly in "Calypso" that the walk round the corner to the porkbutcher's becomes an odyssey in miniature anyway.[16] On his way to the shop Bloom pictured an idyllic land full of "turbaned faces" and "what do you call them: dulcimers" (47). On the way back, thinking of the Agendath Netaim advertisement in the shadow of the "matutinal cloud" that raised the ghost of Stephen's mother (8–9), the "reapparition" that Stephen later blames for his collapse on Mabbot street (545), Bloom accordingly personifies Lake Tiberias as "the grey sunken cunt of the world" (50). The De Quincey passage begins with an evocation of Molly and Milly but soon degenerates into a nightmarish landscape of infertility, a nocturnal reincarnation of the waste land envisioned in "Calypso."

> The voices blend and fuse in clouded silence: silence that is the infinite of space: and swiftly, silently the soul is wafted over regions of cycles of generations that have lived. A region where grey twilight ever descends, never falls on wide sagegreen pasturefields, shedding her dusk, scattering a perennial dew of stars. She follows her mother with ungainly steps, a mare leading her fillyfoal. Twilight phantoms are they yet moulded in prophetic grace of structure, slim shapely haunches, a supple tendonous neck, the meek apprehensive skull. They fade, sad phantoms: all is gone. Agendath is a waste land, a home of screechowls and the sandblind upupa. Netaim, the golden, is no more. And on the highway of the clouds they come, muttering thunder of rebellion, the ghosts of beasts. Huuh! Hark! Huuh! Parallax stalks behind and goads them, the lancinating lightnings of whose brow are scorpions. Elk and yak, the bulls of Bashan and of Babylon, mammoth and mastodon, they come trooping to the sunken sea, *Lacus Mortis*. Ominous, revengeful zodiacal host! They moan, passing upon the clouds, horned and capricorned, the trumpeted with the tusked, the lionmaned and giantlered, snouter and crawler, ruminant and pachyderm, all their moving moaning multitude, murderers of the sun. (338)

The vision of Milly then arises to dispel this gloom the way the imaginary girl came running in the sunlight from Berkeley Road as the cloud passed in "Calypso."

> Onward to the dead sea they tramp to drink, unslaked and with horrible gulpings, the salt somnolent inexhaustible flood. And the equine portent grows again, magnified in the deserted heavens, nay to heaven's own magnitude, till it looms, vast, over the house of Virgo. And lo, wonder of metempsychosis, it is she, the everlasting bride, harbinger of the daystar, the bride, ever virgin. It is she, Martha, thou lost one, Millicent, the young, the dear, the radiant. How serene does she now arise, a queen among the Pleiades, in the penultimate antelucan hours, shod in sandals of bright gold, coifed with a veil of what do you call it gossamer! It floats, it flows about her starborn flesh and loose it streams emerald, sapphire, mauve and heliotrope, sustained on currents of cold interstellar wind, winding, coiling, simply swirling writhing in the skies a mysterious writing till after a myriad metamorphoses of symbol, it blazes, Alpha, a ruby and triangled sign upon the forehead of Taurus. (338)

Only a handful of telltale words like "Agendath," "Netaim," "parallax," "metempsychosis," "Martha" and "Millicent" connect the verbal surface of the passage with Bloom's consciousness. Incidental features of the pasticheur's hyperbole cast us backwards and forwards in the book: the "myriad metamorphoses of symbol" resembles the mocking narrator's "effulgence symbolistic" at the climax of "M'Appari" (227), while the "cold interstellar wind" anticipates the "cold of interstellar space" that the Ithacan catechist will tell us Bloom feels when Stephen leaves 7 Eccles Street (578). And of course the phrases "what do you call it gossamer" and "simply swirling" introduce echoes of Bloom's voice into the sonorous prose, the former recalling the dulcimers associated with the east in "Calypso" and with Simon Dedalus's voice in "Sirens" (225), and the veil of gossamer Gerty's perfume brings to mind (307), the latter invoking Milly and Boylan. The words and phrases that we can ascribe to Bloom offset the portentous language and give the pastiche an awkwardness that is as welcome as the authenticating intrusions of Bloom's voice were amid what would otherwise have been stylistic excess at the climax of "M'Appari" and in the elegiac paragraph in "Nausicaa."

Aside from the sublime quality of Joyce's imitation of De Quincey there are a couple of notable elements that flow against the current of familiarity with Bloom generated by these words and phrases and that actually suggest Stephen's presence. First of all, the language of astrology and the occult here anticipates the Landor imitation. At the conclusion of that paragraph we find Stephen pretending to be an initiate into "the mysteries of karmic law" and pronouncing oracularly upon "planet Alpha of the lunar chain" and "the rubycoloured egos from the second constellation" (340), thus echoing the De Quincey passage with its bestial apparitions that are "zodiacal" and "capricorned," its "house of Virgo" and its transformation of the Bass label into "Alpha, a ruby and triangled sign upon the forehead of Taurus." The second element that distances us from Bloom's awareness and suggests that the voices blending and fusing in the clouded silence are his and Stephen's is the use of epithets reminiscent of the Litany of Our Lady of Loreto ("the everlasting bride, the harbinger of the daystar, the bride, ever virgin") to herald the advent of Milly.[17] Just as the elegiac treatment of Bloom's view of Sandymount and Howth redeemed the cheapened sentiment of Gerty's tale, the effect of the Litany here is to redeem the desecrated Mariolatry of "Nausicaa" in language as exalted as that which characterized the paragraphs about the Elijah skiff in "Wandering Rocks" and the ascent of "ben Bloom Elijah" in "Cyclops."

The vision of Milly is genuine and the juxtaposition of the liturgical and the colloquial is tantalizing, too: the Litany is more likely to be part of the furniture of Stephen's mind, although Milly is Bloom's daughter, his worry, and as such probably the closest thing to a blessed virgin he knows. As a candidate for beatification she is no more worthy than, say, Dilly Dedalus. Nor is Bloom's imagination more mythopoeic than Stephen's. It is the fortuitous conjunction of their worlds that allows this passage to take flight the way it does. Where devices like the pun about "Clan Milly" and the quotations from Bloom's interior monologue weighed down their respective contexts with arbitrary associations, the components of this pastiche form a harmonious whole. The progression from imagery that evokes the deprivation of the Exodus story to a kind of ecstatic comic poetry is startling. The personification of parallax as a goading herdsman and the description of Milly's appearance as a "wonder of metempsychosis" suggest the humorous turn not only of Bloom's mind but of the composition of *Ulysses,* too, while the enhancement of De Quincey's rhythms with the language of Mariolatry, astrology and the occult suggests a transcendence of the negativity of irony and satire like that which was achieved in the descriptions of the Elijah skiff and Bloom's ascent. The sheer copiousness of the verbiage looks forward to the spectacular indulgences of "Circe," "Eumaeus" and "Ithaca."

The initial style was devised to portray Stephen and Bloom separately, so it would not have served to render a real meeting of the two. In "Nausicaa" and "Oxen of the Sun" we can see how Joyce makes the mocking narrator who emerged in "Sirens" and "Cyclops" fit for the task. Of the four examples I selected, only the first and the last were unqualified successes. The mingling of the discourses of Gerty and Bloom subtly prepares us for the formidable symbiosis of the discursive principles represented by Stephen and Bloom in the De Quincey pastiche. The brief panorama of Sandymount and Howth, interspersed with snatches of the initial style, redeems the insincerity of the first part of "Nausicaa." Later the combination of fragments from Bloom's thoughts and the esoteric jargon associated with Stephen results in a strange, extravagant poetry that thoroughly integrates the materials that were hastily joined in the Biblical speech and the Gothic parody. Those two passages demonstrate how Joyce must risk trivializing the psychological and verbal intricacies of his novel if he is to succeed in bringing the text's parodic intelligence to bear upon them. So the cryptic Biblical rhetoric confuses Stephen and Bloom's dreams, and Mulligan's Gothic spoof brazenly recycles phrases they used earlier in the day, but the treatment of Bloom's reverie over the Bass label is different: the fluent Mariolatry and occultism is brilliantly offset by hints of Bloom's voice that legitimate the imitation's poetic license and suggest the humanizing effect he might have on Stephen. Ezra Pound said technique was the test of a writer's sincerity.[18] Surely Joyce satisfies this criterion in "Oxen of the Sun." The series of styles was a providential innovation, not a diversion but an expedient that allowed him to operate unfettered by the decorum a fixed narrator would call for. In "Nausicaa" the Kish lightship and Howth head behold Bloom with a mixture of mischief and inscrutability that foreshadows the inspired play of the next chapter. In the paragraphs in De Quincey's style Bloom's visions of the east are imagined again, as if the melancholy soliloquist of "Proteus" has turned his attention to them and, in doing so, has been magically endowed with the magnanimity he so sorely lacks. So the allusions to the realm of the initial style in "Oxen" open vistas in which we can see the great drama of the book unfolding.[19]

6

"Circe": Stage Directions and Dialogue

This chapter will describe the language of "Circe," the way its two-pronged narrative of stage directions and dialogue functions.[1] "Circe" is the climax that all the parodic voices between "Sirens" and "Oxen of the Sun" have prepared the way for. In the whirlwind of fantasy every narrative convention is revealed to be an artificial construct. But "Circe" is a work of imaginative virtuosity, not a retreat into sterile experimentation; rather than obscuring the literal level of the book's meaning, the verbal sharpness of Joyce's hallucinatory display actually enriches the human drama, contributing immeasurably to our sense of Bloom's world. The visit to Bella Cohen's could not have been recounted in the manner of a story in *Dubliners*—the style of "scrupulous meanness"[2] would not have borne the associative poetic freight that "Circe" carries. In fact the ordinary business of setting and physical description is so completely overshadowed by the production of mythopoeic pyrotechnics that it would be easier to compare the episode to a section in *Finnegans Wake*. Under cover of night places develop human characteristics: the sewers of Mecklenburg Street become the clefts of *"the womancity"* (389). At the same time, the simplest inflections or movements turn people into animals, so we have the streetsmart Zoe spouting *"walrus smoke through her nostrils"* (424) and the meek Bloom greeting the nymph from his bedroom by lifting *"a turtle head towards her lap"* (445). In fact, Stephen's assertion in the opening pages of the chapter that gesture might be a universal language (353) gives us a clue to the method of "Circe."[3] Joyce embraces the conventions of playwriting in order to cloud the formal distinctions that have governed not just his book but prose fiction in general. The breaking down of boundaries releases a torrent of words. It becomes clear that the dramatic framework of dialogue and stage directions merely furnishes the pretext for a spectacle that is often purely verbal. Like "Oxen," "Circe" is a pageant of fictional gestures, stylized narrative poses.

The dramatic format is more like the initial style than the parodic methods of "Cyclops," "Nausicaa" and "Oxen of the Sun," however. The combination of stage directions and dialogue could be compared to the initial style's mechanism of third-person narration and interior monologue, except for the fact that the two components of "Circe" are far more mutable than those of the first nine episodes.[4] This chapter will look at several examples of this new suppleness. For one thing, the distinction between silent meditation and reported speech is often blurred in "Circe": at times Bloom's utterances develop the unmistakable blend of staccato rhythm, truncated grammar and associative logic that characterizes the interior monologue. And, of course, early on in the chapter, the stage directions incorporate the paranoid babble of Bloom's speeches and so blur the distinction between third-person narration and dialogue. These effects are designed to give pause to the reader who presumes that the empirical events of the chapter can be easily separated from the fantasies. There is no single, consistent parodic approach like any of those we find in the previous three episodes, but parodic flourishes abound in the stage directions. As we shall see, for example, the direction that summarizes Bloom's attempt to exonerate himself from the charge of molesting Mary Driscoll is a remarkable flight of fancy that recalls the absurd catalogues of "Cyclops." And yet, unlike most of the interruptions in "Cyclops," the direction supposedly summarizes a speech by Bloom that we never get a chance to hear elsewhere. Even more problematic in some ways are the stage directions I will focus on in the first part of this chapter, the passages that could not really be called parodic but that employ extravagant language to describe things that are obviously illusory. In "Circe" we cannot depend on any of the conventional boundaries we have grown accustomed to.

Here is how the alternative form of narration represented by the parenthesized and italicized directions functions: Bloom's messianic fantasy flowers as Zoe Higgins lures him into Bella's house. The fantasy itself arises from their conversation outside on Tyrone Street. As the young whore accosts him the stage directions betray the peculiar narrative trappings Joyce has cast them in. This episode is so pregnant with figurative language that any stray item of sensory data may blossom into an orgiastic hallucination that belittles the original detail. Zoe and Bloom's exchange triggers a host of exotic associations. He is wary at first, but, dispossessed of his talismanic potato, he begins to respond to her advances.

(She puts the potato greedily into a pocket, then links his arm, cuddling him with supple warmth. He smiles uneasily. Slowly, note by note, oriental music is played. He gazes in the tawny crystal of her eyes, ringed with kohol. His smile softens.)

ZOE

You'll know me the next time.

BLOOM

(Forlornly) I never loved a dear gazelle but it was sure to . . . *(Gazelles are leaping, feeding on the mountains. Near are lakes. Round their shores file shadows black of cedargroves. Aroma rises, a strong hairgrowth of resin. It burns, the orient, a sky of sapphire, cleft by the bronze flight of eagles. Under it lies the womancity, nude, white, still, cool, in luxury. A fountain murmurs among damask roses. Mammoth roses murmur of scarlet winegrapes. A wine of shame, lust, blood exudes, strangely murmuring.)*

ZOE

(*Murmuring singsong with the music, her odalisk lips lusciously smeared with salve of swinefat and rosewater*) Schorach ani wenowach, benoith Hierushaloim.

BLOOM

(*Fascinated*) I thought you were of good stock by your accent.

ZOE

And you know what thought did? (*She bites his ear gently with little goldstopped teeth sending on him a cloying breath of stale garlic. The roses draw apart, disclose a sepulchre of the gold of kings and their mouldering bones.*) (389)

Bloom's strength in "Circe" comes from his acceptance that, for him, the visit to Bella's will be a sojourn in a patriarchal burial ground. He allows himself to be led by Zoe, confident that he will be able to deal with her on his own terms. The three descriptive stage directions here develop a second discourse that runs parallel to the primary narrative the way the musical echoes and the parodic interruptions did in "Sirens" and "Cyclops," respectively.[5] The Oriental music anticipates the overripe landscape Bloom's reference to Moore calls forth. The tropical vista is actually inspired by the *"slim black velvet fillet"* and the *"sapphire slip, closed with three bronze buckles"* (387) that Zoe is wearing. We can see the precise mechanism of this narrative parallelism working when, as Zoe bites Bloom's ear, a final detail is added to the unreal landscape. The stylization of the sepulchral image reflects Bloom's knowledge that he will be able to walk away from whatever Zoe leads him into. On a more literal level, the gold-laiden tomb beneath the roses clearly represents the *"little goldstopped teeth"* (389) behind Zoe's *"dumb moist lips"* (388). Joyce uses the stage directions to clothe the action of the episode in figurative language. Zoe's Eastern aura is evoked so copiously here that, even after thirteen pages of Bloom's messianic fantasy, it only takes a few touches of metaphor and epithet to recreate it as she continues to solicit in her sultry proverbial way.[6]

ZOE

Silent means consent. (*With little parted talons she captures his hand her forefinger giving to his palm the passtouch of secret monitor, luring him to doom*) Hot hands cold gizzard.
(*He hesitates amid scents, music, temptations. She leads him towards the steps, drawing him by the odour of her armpits, the vice of her painted eyes, the rustle of her slip in whose sinuous folds lurks the lion reek of all the male brutes that have possessed her.*)

THE MALE BRUTES

(*Exhaling sulphur of rut and dung and ramping in their loosebox, faintly roaring, their drugged heads swaying to and fro*) Good! (409)

These brutes come from a jungle world that is not Bloom's natural habitat; it is the place Virag describes to him where woman "offers her allmoist yoni to man's lingam" (424). Bloom is no more at home with such a vision than he is with the nymph's "stonecold" purity (449). Although they are far from representing a golden mean, Bloom's peculiar sexual tastes are neither completely brutal nor completely Platonic. Zoe herself embodies an aspect of the Eastern seductress from the dream Bloom recalled in "Nausicaa" (303, 311–12), as well as a creature from his lost youth, the "dear gazelle" of the valentine he sent Josie Powell (363). In a more subtle and general way her overtures reawaken the longing for Oriental repose he felt in "Calypso" and "Lotus Eaters" (47, 58–59). But the extravagant presentation of Zoe and the desire she arouses in Bloom also incorporates an element from the bookstall vignette in "Wandering Rocks" where the lush prose of *Sweets of Sin* brings aromas of "Armpits' oniony sweat" and "Sulphur dung of lions" (194) to Bloom's flared nostrils. Still, having masturbated, he is now able to resist the temptation and, later, of course, he uses this very language to rebuff Bella after he has taken the nymph to task (452). Despite Bloom's ability to distance himself from it now, the style of *Sweets of Sin* is clearly a precedent for the luxuriant eroticism we find in some of the stage directions. The heroine of the novel gives Raoul a kiss that is *"luscious,"* like Zoe's *"odalisk lips."* Again, the heroine's *"opulent curves"* are projected onto Molly when she appears on the edge of nighttown dressed in the Turkish breeches of Bloom's dream (359). Even ostensibly innocuous images are contaminated by this style: for instance, when Bloom defends himself against the Mary Driscoll charge he speaks of mending his ways in the *"bosom of the family,"* which he describes as *"heaving"* like the heroine's *"embonpoint"* in *Sweets of Sin* (194, 377). This echoing of half-forgotten phrases adds to the secondhand quality of the homely wishes, regrets and embarrassments that the episode magnifies so grotesquely, reminding us that Bloom's imagination, like Stephen's, is a mass of quotations.

The paragraph describing Bloom's entrance illustrates the sheer mutability that will distinguish the stage directions from the other narrative structures in the book. We are made to see just how potent Joyce's style can be. At the same time though we realize that all the verbal gymnastics eventually bring us back to the simple fact of Bloom's humanity. The language of "Circe" is spectacular because it dramatizes the liberating collapse of formal constraints. For example, the mercurial tone of the following passage demonstrates that the episode involves not only the full arsenal of Joyce's narrative techniques but the ironic intelligence that allows him to perceive the limitations of style as well. The scene is being set. Stephen and Lynch pass, and Bloom appears.

(They pass. Tommy Caffrey scrambles to a gaslamp and, clasping, climbs in spasms. From the top spar he slides down. Jacky Caffrey clasps to climb. The navvy lurches against the lamp. The twins scuttle off in the dark. The navvy, swaying, presses a forefinger against a wing of

his nose and ejects from the farther nostril a long liquid jet of snot. Shouldering the lamp he staggers away through the crowd with his flaring cresset.

Snakes of river fog creep slowly. From drains, clefts, cesspools, middens arise on all sides stagnant fumes. A glow leaps in the south beyond the seaward reaches of the river. The navvy staggering forward cleaves the crowd and lurches toward the tramsiding. On the farther side under the railway bridge Bloom appears flushed, panting, cramming bread and chocolate into a side pocket. From Gillen's hairdresser's window a composite portrait shows him gallant Nelson's image. A concave mirror at the side presents to him lovelorn longlost lugubru Booloohoom. Grave Gladstone sees him level, Bloom for Bloom. He passes, struck by the stare of truculent Welling-on but in the convex mirror grin unstruck the bonham eyes and fatchuck cheekchops of Jollypoldy the rixdix doldy.

At Antonio Rabaiotti's door Bloom halts, sweated under the bright arclamps. He disappears. In a moment he reappears and hurries on.) (354)

The transition from what sounds like good action writing to wordplay is remarkable here. The piglike *"fatchuck cheekchops"* foreshadow the Circean Bello that Bloom calls "Empress" (432) and remind us that the masochistic fantasy will be the real adventure of the episode. The first sentences in the passage quoted above combine the Gothic atmospherics of the fiery horizon and the drunken torchbearer with the squalid lyricism of the navvy's *"long liquid jet of snot."* With the *"snakes of river fog"* and the *"stagnant fumes"* portentous effects ripen into the sort of rich language that will characterize the exchange with Zoe.[7] The personification of the river fog and the inclusion of the general term "clefts" among the particulars of *"drains,"* *"cesspools"* and *"middens"* foreshadows the musings on the "cloven sex" and their fear of "creeping things" that Virag elicits from Bloom (421). The real setting of "Circe" is the streets of *"the woman-city,"* after all: like "Oxen of the Sun," it is a narrative in which all discourses lead to the sexual realm. Still, although the hallucinatory method is perceptibly gearing up as Bloom enters, we sense that he will pass through this stylistic hall of mirrors unscathed.[8] He will not be purged of his afflictions; neither beatified nor damned, he will remain essentially the same. The juxtaposition of Bloom's Chaplinesque figure with the solemn images of Nelson, Gladstone and Wellington is nevertheless appropriate, since his rescue of his friend's son is as meaningful as any of their accomplishments. The announcement of Bloom's arrival acts as a pivot between the setting of the hallucinatory scene and the excursion into kaleidoscopic wordplay that *"Gillen's hairdresser's window"* provokes. The heterogeneous components of the passage are all attuned to one another. The three paragraphs hold the suspenseful, the comic and the musical in a nice balance that reflects the equanimity we associate with Bloom. His entrance dissipates the suspense created by the fiery horizon and the drunken torchbearer and brings playful intimations of the phantasmagoria to come. The music of *"lovelorn longlost lugubru Booloohoom"* and *"Jollypoldy the rixdix doldy"* has charms that offset the perfunctory alliteration and assonance of gallant Nelson appearing in Gillen's window and Bloom being *"struck by the stare of truculent Wellington."* It is

Bloom's sympathetic presence that puts the melodramatic setting in perspective and inspires the siren music of the concave and convex mirror images.

The sense of possibility opened up by the episode's stylistic variety and surrealism is of a piece with the wild atmosphere of the location and the hour. The dreaming spirit of exaggeration and digression eventually reveals truth of a different order from that which the daylight episodes yielded. In fact the text of "Circe" resembles the initial style in the teasing way that dreams recall reality. There is a shimmer of falseness in the stage manager's echoes of the initial style's third-person narrator. Consider these directions from Bello's humiliation of the womanly Bloom, for example.

(Milly Bloom, fairhaired, greenvested, slimsandalled, her blue scarf in the seawind simply swirling, breaks from the arms of her lover and calls, her young eyes wonderwide.) (442)

Out of her oak frame a nymph with hair unbound, lightly clad in teabrown art colours, descends from her grotto and passing under interlacing yews, stands over Bloom. (444)

(Through silversilent summer air the dummy of Bloom, rolled in a mummy, rolls rotatingly from the Lion's Head cliff into the purple waiting waters.) (449)

The density of detail in these sentences marks them as momentary apparitions. All three occur in the emotional center of the episode which, if only it were a little more solemn and spare, would almost amount to a Beckettian exploration of secret memories and forbidden desires. Milly appears when Bello tells Bloom "there's a man of brawn in possession" at 7 Eccles Street and turns him into Rip Van Winkle in a cruel dramatization of his thoughts of his courtship in "Nausicaa" (308–9). The nymph descends after Bello has had Bloom sacrificed on a suttee pyre, while the dummy falls as the encounter with the nymph nears its conclusion. As artificial reproductions of the familiar tone of the morning hours, these sentences capture the narrative in a transitional stage between that clarity and the vagaries of the nocturnal world as they manifest themselves in "Eumaeus" and "Ithaca."

We may chafe against the unreality at this point and wonder if such vagaries will bear any fruit. However, this artificiality is the quality that enables "Circe" to bridge the gap between the morning world and the homecoming chapters. "Wandering Rocks" forms a similar link between the initial style and the parodic voices of "Sirens" and "Cyclops." Like the interpolated sentences in "Wandering Rocks" the stage directions quoted above come from nowhere and create a sense of constant movement. However, the blatancy of their unreality prevents them from achieving the triumphant style that distinguished the Elijah skiff's passage down the Liffey. Indeed Bloom prompts this comparison himself by murmuring "Giddy Elijah" as he thinks of falling from the cliff (448). These sentences do not achieve the sensuousness of the figurative language Zoe's entrance was couched in, because, although they do recall it, especially the mannered diction used to evoke *"the womancity,"* they are discrete imaginary flashes that do not gel as a coherent pattern of imagery the way that language did.

What makes these sentences noteworthy is their anticipation of the peculiar grammatical drift of "Eumaeus" and "Ithaca." We read the directions quoted above as rather hollow set-pieces and this perception reinforces the claim made by the parodic episodes that no narrative technique can do full justice to any empirical world it seeks to represent. The fictional machinations of "Circe" have been designed to illustrate states of mind: the vision of Rudy is a fictive imitation of Bloom's paternal feeling as he watches over Stephen. So "Circe" cultivates the premise that was established in the narratives of "Sirens," "Cyclops," "Nausicaa" and "Oxen of the Sun," and which will be explored in a far less consistently parodic way through the severely qualified realism and poetic comedy of the late night episodes.

As always, of course, the formal dimension has a psychological counterpart. The moral thrust of this drama proceeds from the supposition that fantasy neutralizes the embarrassing secrets we keep for the better part of our waking lives: the need to daydream is related to the fictive impulse.[9] Bloom is the author of the humiliation which, by and large, he relishes. Each of the directions quoted above touches upon a detail from the wanderings of the morning, using a hallucinatory shorthand of compound words and remembered phrases. The description of Milly brings together the girl with "slim sandals" and "gold hair" who comes running in the sunlight from Berkeley Road (50) and the Jew's daughter "all dressed in green" who beheads little Harry Hughes in the song Stephen sings for Bloom later (565–67). With a similar stroke the *"teabrown art colours"* identify the nymph as the subject of the *Photo Bits* picture over the Blooms' bed (53) while the site of the dummy's fall is clearly the Howth of Bloom's reverie in Davy Byrne's (144). In each instance the wording betrays the illusory nature of the image. The fact that the purple depths off Lion's Head cliff are *"waiting"* for the dummy is indicative of the direction's crass theatricality. The cloying prettiness of the "teabrown art colours" is registered in order to prepare us for the nymph's moral falseness.[10] In the case of the apparition of Milly the alliteration is a subliminal signal. The automated, pseudo-poetic repetitiousness here looks forward to the exhausted and exhaustive outpourings of "Eumaeus" and "Ithaca," respectively. In those episodes Joyce deliberately includes mechanical flaws like alliteration and rhyme that other prose writers would eliminate as a matter of course. Thus in the studied shabbiness of "Eumaeus" we find sentences like, "Mr Bloom, so far as he was personally concerned, was just pondering in pensive mood" (514), in which the alliteration is as facile as that of the *"slimsandalled"* Milly with *"her blue scarf in the seawind simply swirling."* Of course the ramshackle style in which the next chapter's weary equivocations are presented is no more authentic than the transparent unreality of this one; the point is just that "Circe" is the vortex towards which all the expansive styles of *Ulysses* tend. As for the perverse singsong rhyme of *"the dummy of Bloom, rolled in a mummy,"* the Ithacan catechist makes a virtue of this quirk by filling his obsessively symmetrical catalogues with drolleries like this statement about Milly's genetic make-up: "blond, born of two dark, she had blond ancestry, remote, a violation, Herr Hauptmann Hainau, Austrian army, proximate, a hallucination, lieutenant Mulvey, British navy" (568).

There is an undertow of facetiousness in "Ithaca" that strains against the reassuring flow of information and warns us of the folly of accepting the urbane questions and answers too readily. The rhyming of "violation" and "hallucination" here links the supposedly factual catechism to the fantasies of nighttown, since the Latinate words only elaborate the stage direction's more rudimentary rhythm.

A number of factors keep the surreal mechanization of the stage directions in check: the presence of the primary cast of characters in Bella's parlor, the voices of Stephen and Bloom, the salty talk of the girls. It is Bloom's voice though, and the recognizable contents of his mind, that steadies the episode's careening farce. His interior monologue in particular is the metronome behind the comic orchestration. Similarly, in "Eumaeus" the familiar patterns of Bloom's speech and thought give definition to the style's verbal slippage. In "Circe" Bloom appears to be thinking aloud when he first enters. It is fitting that the colloquial part of the initial style should gain ascendancy in "Circe," where the relaxation of formal constraints leads to a proliferation of spoken words. At first I detect only a vague reminiscence of the interior monologue in the narrative summary of Bloom's speech. For example, when Molly appears the parenthesized italics contain this sentence: *"He breathes in deep agitation, swallowing gulps of air, questions, hopes, crubeens for her supper, things to tell her, excuses, desire, spellbound"* (359).

"Sirens" contained analogous combinations of third-person narration and Bloom's voice. The shards of interior monologue in the mocking narrator's discourse at the climax of "M'Appari" are comparable to the two central phrases here (*"crubeens for her supper, things to tell her"*) which, despite the third-person pronouns, more closely approximate something Bloom might be supposed to have said to Molly than the rest of the sentence does. Such glossing of dialogue is elementary to the craft of fiction, but at this point in "Circe" the confusion prepares the way for Bloom's response to the shade of Mrs. Breen on the following page, in which the less tractable distinction between silent meditation and directly reported speech is blurred. She castigates him for being in nighttown and he says: "Not so loud my name. Whatever do you think me? Don't give me away. Walls have hears. How do you do? It's ages since I. You're looking splendid. Absolutely it. Seasonable weather we are having this time of year. Black refracts heat. Short cut home here. Interesting quarter. Rescue of fallen women Magdalen asylum. I am the secretary" (362).

The gossipy tone in the body of the speech marks the first emergence of the feminized Bloom. Still, the way the speech tapers off into telegraphed babble recalls the interior monologue. At this point in the chapter it seems that new formal oddities are being improvised at every turn to accommodate the deepening hallucinatory comedy. Consider the incongruous shape of Bloom's "bogus statement" in the Mary Driscoll case, a passage that builds upon the clouded distinctions in the two previous quotations.

> *(Bloom, pleading not guilty and holding a fullblown waterlily, begins a long unintelligible speech. They would hear what counsel had to say in his stirring address to the grandjury. He was down and out but, though branded as a black sheep, if he might say so, he meant to reform, to retrieve the memory of the past in a purely sisterly way and return to nature as a purely domestic animal. A seven months' child, he had been carefully brought up and nurtured by an aged bedridden parent. There might have been lapses of an erring father but he wanted to turn over a new leaf and now, when at long last in sight of the whipping post, to lead a homely life in the evening of his days, permeated by the affectionate surrounding of the heaving bosom of the family. An acclimatised Britisher, he had seen that summer eve from the footplate of an engine cab of the Loop line railway company while the rain refrained from falling glimpses, as it were, through the windows of loveful households in Dublin city and urban district of scenes truly rural of happiness of the better land with Dockrell's wallpaper at one and ninepence a dozen, innocent Britishborn bairns lisping prayers to the Sacred Infant, youthful scholars grappling with their pensums, model young ladies playing on the pianoforte or anon all with fervour reciting the family rosary round the crackling Yulelog while in the boreens and green lanes the colleens with their swains strolled what times the strains of the organtoned melodeon Britannia metalbound with four acting stops and twelvefold bellows, a sacrifice, greatest bargain ever. . . .)*
> (376–77)

The main confusion here is between summarized speech and parodic writing. We seem to be reading the gloss of a speech, but the grammatical contours of these sentences are revealing. Bloom appears to be desperately and involuntarily telling a series of preposterous lies. The implications of this comic spectacle are poignant. The question of whether or not he would have strung together such a garbled collection of falsehoods is immaterial. We have here an acutely incompetent account of Bloom's life and aspirations, a fiction contrived of scattershot clichés. Still, through the amusing flaws in the fictive screen we can discern the truth of Bloom's unhappiness.

The passage can be divided into two parts, each of which suggests an aspect of that melancholy. His sexual frustration colors the three sentences that recount the story of his life. The testimony sounds ludicrously feeble, but, as the clichés begin to burst with innuendo, we can see how expedient they are. The talk of domestic animals and whipping posts, sisterly ways and heaving bosoms, is seamlessly joined to the contrite pledges to retrieve the memory of the past, return to nature and turn over a new leaf. The platitudes have been arranged so that they foretell the way the femininity we detected in the exchange with Mrs. Breen will turn to masochism in Bella's music room. So the summary of Bloom's speech becomes intelligible once we are able to read the meaningful inappropriateness of its hackneyed vocabulary. The protestations of the accused about his noble aspirations, recorded in the last rambling sentence, actually reveal the genuine displacement felt by this immigrant's son who, although he can quote the price of Dockrell's wallpaper and make a sales pitch for *"the organtoned melodeon Britannia metalbound with four acting stops and twelvefold bellows,"* lacks the verbal skills to avoid the greeting-card doggerel that makes up most of the sentence. The confusion of religion and commerce that leads to the use of the word *"sacrifice"* in the sales pitch is particularly telling. The description of *"the colleens with their swains"* strolling *"in the boreens and green lanes"* to *"the strains of the organtoned melodeon"* far surpasses the mechanical rhyming I have noted in the hallucinations from the encounter with Bello. The patronizing images of Irishness follow logically from the picture of *"innocent Britishborn bairns lisping prayers to the Sacred Infant"* and *"reciting the family rosary,"* which mixes British, Scottish and Catholic labels in a cultural hodgepodge.[11] The hilarious linguistic laxity anticipates "Eumaeus," but the baldness of the burlesque here would not allow for the engaging garrulousness of the next chapter. This is a caricature of alienation: the rider on the footplate of the engine cab who looks in the windows of the *"loveful households in Dublin city and urban district"* to see *"scenes truly rural of happiness"* represents a comic exaggeration like those of the Ithacan problem that reduces Bloom to "eccentric public laughingstock" and "moribund lunatic pauper" (596). And yet this bizarre parodic flourish, like the convolutions of "Oxen," uncovers a morsel of truth about Bloom's character that might otherwise have been lost. Such revelatory verbal clowning locates the narrative of "Circe" squarely between the novel's parodic middle and the qualified realism of the homecoming.

The extraordinary machinations of "Circe" dramatize the observation Bloom made in the newspaper office that everything "speaks in its own way" (100). In nighttown everything does speak: the soap in Bloom's pocket (360), the gulls he fed (370), even the wreaths of smoke and the kisses the whores blow (369, 387), all are given the equivalent of comic-book balloons containing onomatopoeic or vaudevillian near-nonsense. This absurd proliferation of voices underlines the fact that the episode's frenetic movement is more verbal than physical. And of course it is not only inanimate objects that are charged with unearthly power but buried guilts and desires as well. Perhaps the most tangible result of the linguistic virtuosity in "Circe" is the increased articulateness it affords Bloom himself. In the music room, as our voyage through the recesses of his psyche continues, the magical atmosphere bestows expressive gifts upon Bloom, poetic powers that enable him to transcend the incompetence of his *"unintelligible speech"* from the dock. An abundance of keenly felt memories rushes forth as he prepares to be transformed into Ruby Cohen.[12] When the Minnie Hauck fan invites him to tie Bella's bootlace his reminiscences have a dreamlike lucidity: "I can make a true black knot. Learned when I served my time and worked the mail order line for Kellet's. . . . To be a shoefitter in Mansfield's was my love's young dream'' (431–32).

Then, as the yews from *The Bath of the Nymph* taunt him about his adolescence, there is the nostalgic cry: "Let's ring all the bells in Montague Street" (447). More important than these wonderful details, however, is the new eloquence with which Bloom expresses the regrets that have burdened him all day. Outside earlier on he responded to the apparitions of Molly, Mrs. Breen and Mary Driscoll by babbling and lying, but now, in the house, confronted by Lipoti Virag and Bella, he speaks of his misgivings and of his sneaking awareness that this will have been an exceptional day in his life. His grandfather's scoffs at his teenage vow to devote "an entire year to the study of the religious problem" and "the summer months of 1882 to square the circle" and his taste for "women in male habiliments" provoke this touching reply: "I wanted then to have now concluded. Nightdress was never. Hence this. But tomorrow is a new day will be. Past was is today. What now is will then tomorrow as now was be past yester" (420).

Vulnerability and resilience are combined here in a compression of tenses that reflects both the gravity of Bloom's trials and the wisdom of his assumption that they will pass.[13] Readers who think "Circe" nothing more than cynical blustering farce would do well to consider such human poetry. "Circe" treats the point at which dirty talk becomes *"lovewords"* (462). Bloom's interrogators share his fluency too. As Bella approaches, her fan's constructions are similarly monosyllabic and adept: "Is me her was you dreamed before? Was then she him you us since knew? Am all them and the same now me?" (430).

Bloom must feel as if he is about to crawl into eternity across Bella's floor. Far more than Zoe then, Bella reactivates the dream of the seductress in Turkish breeches. Her presence awakens a feverish masochistic passion in him and he waxes poetic once again: "Exuberant female. Enormously I desiderate your domination. I am exhausted, abandoned, no more young. I stand, so to speak, with an unposted letter bearing the extra regulation fee before the too late box of the general postoffice of human life" (430).

Bloom overstates his feelings of weariness and desolation, but it is from this bathetic matrix that the forlorn lyricism of the postal conceit arises. These startling glimmers of insight in the center of the phantasmagoria show what a fundamental necessity the seemingly capricious stylistic variety and surrealism of the episode is. Since Bloom will not emerge from this drama purged of his afflictions, the fact that the episode's form permits him to give expression to them in such memorable ways is significant and consoling.

The action of "Circe" is mostly verbal then. Joyce uses dramatic conventions to illuminate the root of his fictive impulse. In many ways "Circe" is the stylistic zenith of *Ulysses,* the spectacle for which all the earlier techniques are merely preparatory exercises. There seems no end to what the stage directions and dialogue can do, so potently do they combine figurative and colloquial language. More than any other episode in the book, it anticipates *Finnegans Wake* in its exploitation of the protean connotation, the chimerical turn of phrase. In this drama of the *"hobgoblin"* (413) and the *"mirage"* (359), a higher premium is placed on poetic association than ever before. The device of theatrical writing bestows a new legitimacy on material that might have had only a glancing impact in the evocative musings of the interior monologue: that is, when we are told in an italicized stage direction that the grotesque version of Punch Costello has an *"Ally Sloper nose"* (413) or that Bella flirts her *"black horn fan like Minnie Hauch in Carmen"* (429), the detail is mythologized in a way that it would not have been had it come to us through the less auspicious medium of the interior monologue.[14] The dramatic format gives Joyce, if not objectivity, the freedom he desires to glorify or degrade Bloom with a stroke.[15] Thus one moment he is "Ruby Cohen" (436), Bella's novice, then the next he is revealed as Haroun al Raschid (440, 478) travelling incognito, the Arabian mentor of Stephen's dream (39). And of course the ultimate objective of all this deft artifice is to harness the tide of Bloom's sexuality, so the topography of nighttown becomes the anatomy of *"the womancity."* First we have Bloom approaching *"hellsgates"* (367) in Mabbot Street. Then we have him, as Mrs. Miriam Dandrade, clipping his "backgate hairs" (437) to be violated by a distinguished series of men. Later it is *"Beaver Street"* (479) where Cunty Kate and Biddy the Clap watch Stephen's altercation with Private Carr whose obscenities in turn introduce a Miltonic variation of the cloacal motif by unleashing *"Pandemonium"* (488). So, with the format of "Circe," Joyce can make the poetic and the profane cohere in a miraculous way.

In the vision of Rudy we see the crowning achievement of this expressionism. The tenderness of the paternal tableau vindicates all the distortions of the dramatic method. We can sense the irony subsiding as Bloom first mishears "Who Goes with Fergus," then murmurs the Masonic oath, and at last, transcending his incompetence once again, utters the phrases that give the vision its Dantean dimension: "in the rough sands of the sea . . . a cabletow's length from the shore . . . where the tide ebbs . . . and flows" (497).

Although the allusion, if there is one, has not been traced, there is song in those words.[16] The wanderer is nearing the rock of Ithaca. The seafaring imagery recalls the "homing" *Rosevean* at the end of part 1 (42). It seems clear also that, in the dreamy incantatory murmuring, we are invited to hear an echo of Dante's immersion in Lethe at the climax of the *Purgatorio.*[17] The resonant phrases serve as an introductory movement for the stage direction that follows, establishing just the right note of exhausted rapture. *"(Silent, thoughtful, alert, he stands on guard, his fingers at his lips in the attitude of secret master. Against the dark wall a figure appears slowly, a fairy boy of eleven, a changeling, kidnapped, dressed in an Eton suit with glass shoes and a little bronze helmet, holding a book in his hand. He reads from right to left inaudibly, smiling, kissing the page)"* (497).

So, after the reassuring banality of the exchange with Corny Kelleher, one last, climactic vision arises. Bloom's attitude, which recalls not only Zoe's *"passtouch of secret monitor"* (409) but also the Masonic signs he gave earlier (372, 429), causes an air of occult solemnity to prevail. In fact he seems to will this pathetically idealized apparition into existence. The episode closes then with the momentary exaltation of Bloom's mind in creation like Shelley's fading coal. The sonless father's call may be inaudible, but it is a formidable curtain line, and we must assume that the sugary details of the picture correspond to the quality of Bloom's yearning as he watches over Stephen.[18] As is always the case in "Circe," the dimensions of the narrative language are prescribed by the vagaries of the character's mind. "Circe" is a mosaic of such gestures, bringing to life *"body phantoms"* (410), like those that left the footmarks on Bella's oilcloth floor-covering, and taking place in the *"nebulous obscurity"* (413) that occupies space when Florry Talbot crosses herself in preparation for the end of the world. The vision of Rudy is not so much a conclusion as a conclusive gesture, as arbitrary and as final as the full stop at the end of "Ithaca." As we soon learn in "Eumaeus," Stephen has not been transfigured and Bloom has not been redeemed.[19] It is just that, for the moment, the amoebic stage directions have assumed a shape that resembles that of a tidily wrapped-up story. But no one lives happily ever after and the story is not even over. All that has happened is that Russell's criterion for a work of art has been satisfied: a "spiritual essence" (152) from the depths of Bloom's unfulfilled life has been given form. Still, the essence returns to invisibility as the transparent lamp passes away and the spiritual flame flickers out.[20] Bloom's renewed incompetence will cast a long shadow over the narrative of "Eumaeus."

When Joyce finished "Circe" he thought it was the best thing he had ever written.[21] In fact, as I have suggested, the journey through Bloom's unconscious marks the emergence of the author of *Finnegans Wake*. In terms of the narrative strategies of *Ulysses* the dramatic format can be seen as a kind of inside-out version of the initial style: there is a diminution in the exactness of that style's third-person narrator and a correspondent ballooning of the associative properties of the interior monologue, so that Bloom's psyche, gradually and in momentary spasms, attains the fecundity of an artist's.[22] After all this, readers are prepared for the less-flamboyant subversions of narrative decorum in "Eumaeus" and "Ithaca."

The Narrative Treachery of "Eumaeus"

The narrative of "Eumaeus" wanders along clownishly like an imitation of conventional realistic fiction in which the omissions and equivocations are the most bewitching features. Verbose, colloquial, gritty and amusing in an offbeat way, the episode derives its appeal from the obvious relish with which Joyce lets himself slip into the pitfalls facing any writer of prose narratives. Only a lord of language could make such negative effort an occasion for delight.[1] There is a sense of winding down in "Eumaeus" though, a feeling of letting go that is particularly welcome after the relentless pyrotechnics of the last few episodes. Our delight is not immediate, of course. At first the avalanche of cliché, solecism and inelegant variation seems all too monolithic, as if in his bid for incompetent anonymity Joyce had actually absolved himself of the obligation to entertain us. Eventually, however, we learn to perceive modulations in the seeming stylelessness. Consider the account of D. B. Murphy's entry into the conversation, for example:

> The redbearded sailor who had his weather eye on the newcomers boarded Stephen, whom he had singled out for attention in particular, squarely by asking:
> —And what might your name be?
> Just in the nick of time Mr Bloom touched his companion's boot but Stephen, apparently disregarding the warm pressure from an unexpected quarter, answered:
> —Dedalus.
> The sailor stared at him heavily from a pair of drowsy baggy eyes, rather bunged up from excessive use of boose, preferably good old Hollands and water.
> —You know Simon Dedalus? he asked at length.
> —I've heard of him, Stephen said. (509)

The simplicity and clarity here is odd. The narrative business is managed with an economy and accuracy of detail that will be a sporadic feature of the episode. Even so, the narrative still seems a little out of joint when the phrase "just in the nick of time" is used to describe a warning gesture that goes completely unheeded. The phrase is not just another cliché: it is one sign of the very real but unfulfilled sense of adventure in the episode.[2] In "Eumaeus" the book's customary affection for the quotidian threatens to become a veritable romance of squalid subculture. This is the episode where Bloom and Stephen are described

as "our two noctambules" (508) as if they were figures of the Parisian under-
world, where Murphy's departure to urinate is elevated to the level of "an incident" (521) and where, at the end, the entire scene in the shelter is referred to
as "the séance" (539), as if Joyce had used a Ouija board to conjure up the keeper
who may be Skin-the-Goat, the dissipated cabby who may be the Parnellite Henry
Campbell and even the sailor who calls himself D. B. Murphy. This romance
of the squalid accounts for the adjectival slackness in the evocation of the sailor's
"drowsy baggy eyes." The deliberately guileless lyricism here will be a recurring element in the episode, too. Many of the scene's memorable images are
formed by such double constructions. The "boiling swimming cup" of coffee
the keeper brings (509), the whore of the lane's "demented glassy grin" (517),
Stephen's sensation of Bloom's "sinewless and wobbly" arm guiding him (539),
all of these are testimony to the narrator's ready verbal generosity. Finally, in
the passage above, we have the curious manner in which the omniscience of the
narrator is suggested; with the phrase "preferably good old Hollands and water"
it is revealed that he knows something about Murphy's habits. The arbitrary inclusion of the detail does not, as we might expect, draw attention to the artificiality
of the fictional fabric but rather reinforces our impression that we are reading
about real people. The narrator seems even to endorse Murphy's preference.[3]

"Eumaeus" has the appearance of a hastily written document rather than
a work of art composed in tranquility. The battered language has a certain
malleability though, an emotional residue that is entirely absent form the legalistic
style of "Ithaca." The question of the cuckold's response to his dilemma is a
case in point. In "Eumaeus" two improbable scenarios are dramatized with comic
verve while the Ithacan catechism merely includes the outlandish in a methodical
list of options. The first of these scenarios in "Eumaeus" is sketched when Bloom
reflects upon his grudging admiration for those who use physical force to achieve
political ends, the second when he considers how much more he knows about
adultery than the cabbies who chat with such ease about Parnell's relationship
with Kitty O'Shea. For my purpose it is worth extracting the two vignettes from
their wordy surroundings in order to compare them as alternate versions of the
betrayed husband's confrontation with his unfaithful wife.

> Those love vendettas of the south, have her or swing for her, when the husband frequently,
> after some words passed between the two concerning her relations with the other lucky mortal
> (he having had the pair watched), inflicted fatal injuries on his adored one as a result of an
> alternative postnuptial *liaison* by plunging his knife into her. (525)

> A domestic rumpus and the erring fair one begging forgiveness of her lord and master upon
> her knees and promising to sever the connection and not receive his visits any more if only
> the aggrieved husband would overlook the matter and let bygones be bygones with tears in her
> eyes though possibly with her tongue in her fair cheek at the same time as quite possibly there
> were several others. (535)

There is no likelihood of anything like either of these situations occurring between Bloom and Molly. The descriptions seem as far from being representations of Bloom's thought processes as any of the hallucinations in "Circe," and yet, without a framing device like the previous episode's blatantly artificial dramatic conventions, these images materialize almost imperceptibly in the desultory prose. The language is not Bloom's, but his consciousness hovers somewhere in the offing. The "love vendetta of the south" is described not long after he mentions Molly's Spanish blood to Stephen and so it can be related to the notion he expresses then of passionate Mediterraneans who "are given to taking the law into their own hands" (520). The marvelously cynical description of the "domestic rumpus" is outlined while Stephen is viewing the photograph of Molly and Bloom is trying to convince himself that adultery is a fact of life. Both of these examples show how the hackneyed narration can offer only very rough approximations of the meanderings of Bloom's mind without really reproducing the immediacy of his voice. Compared to the treatment of the same theme in "Ithaca" though, this relative distance between the narrator and Bloom seems negligible. The catechism is far more arid and droll as Bloom lies beside Molly taking stock of the new development in their relationship.

What retribution, if any?

Assassination, never, as two wrongs did not make one right. Duel by combat, no. Divorce, not now. Exposure by mechanical artifice (automatic bed) or individual testimony (concealed ocular witness), not yet. Suit for damages by legal influence or simulation of assault with evidence of injuries sustained (selfinflicted), not impossibly. Hushmoney by moral influence, possibly. If any, positively, connivance, introduction of emulation (material, a prosperous rival agent of publicity: moral, a successful rival agent of intimacy), depreciation, alienation, humiliation, separation, protecting the one separated from the other, protecting the separator from both. (603)

The terms are ludicrously clinical for such a fiercely human embroilment: instead of "having . . . the pair watched" we speak of a "concealed ocular witness," a proposition that is still less bizarre than the "mechanical artifice" of an "automatic bed." Viewed from this almost otherworldly perspective the drift away from the language of Bloom's consciousness in "Eumaeus" seems less considerable.

As mannered or qualified realism, the style of "Eumaeus" suggests some indeterminate border area between the interior monologue and the parodic voices of "Cyclops," "Nausicaa" and "Oxen of the Sun."[4] The contrived flatness of the prose is leavened now and again by pockets of seemingly inadvertent wit, such as the assertion that Bloom "cordially disliked" policemen (502) and his belief that there are plenty of wives "on for a flutter in polite debauchery" (535). The sparkle of such phrases is enhanced by the functional mediocrity of so much of the narrative. They come as pleasant surprises. Similarly, traces of Cyclopean interruptions, of the fictional imitations of "Oxen" and even of the fantasies of "Circe" can be found here and there, divested of much of their comic flamboyance so as not to rupture the episode's impersonal façade. Here the parodies, pastiches and hallucinations of the earlier styles enter an artless half-life that is the inverse of those moments in the interior monologue when the language outruns Bloom and creates an embryonic version of the later parodic aberrations. For instance, in "Hades" when the carriage passes the site of the Childs murder Bloom's thoughts begin to resemble sensationalistic press clippings. "They looked. Murderer's ground. It passed darkly. Shuttered, tenantless, unweeded garden. Whole place gone to hell. Wrongfully condemned. Murder. The murderer's image in the eye of the murdered. They love reading about it. Man's head found in a garden. Her clothing consisted of. How she met her death. Recent outrage. The weapon used. Murderer is still at large. Clues. A shoelace. The body to be exhumed. Murder will out" (82–83). Or again, in "Lestrygonians" the sight of the *Irish Times* offices causes Bloom to spin out a meticulously imagined list of small ads: "Best paper by a long chalks for a small ad. Got the provinces now. Cook and general, exc. cuisine, housemaid kept. Wanted live man for spirit counter. Resp. girl (R.C.) wishes to hear of post in fruit or pork shop" (131).

In each case it is possible to see something other than the transcription of Bloom's thoughts threatening to emerge. The sense of the print media here enables us to read the latter part of each passage as if it were a series of newspaper clippings pasted together. The first quotation specifically anticipates the Gothic parody in "Oxen," of course, while the second contains the tiniest beginnings of the hilarious list of housing ads in *Finnegans Wake*.[5] Mere shadows of the later flourishes, these comic touches do not disrupt the realism of the initial style. In "Eumaeus" there are analogously faint reminiscences of the parodic episodes when Murphy's fantastic talk causes the scene in the shelter to recede behind clouds of prose that contain imperfect reproductions of Bloom's reveries on the subject of travel. One such paragraph deals with Murphy's imminent return to his wife in Cork. Like the "love vendetta" and the "domestic rumpus" I have just discussed, it is a vision of adultery which springs from Bloom's thoughts but which has a fictive life of its own.

> Mr Bloom could easily picture his advent on this scene, the homecoming to the mariner's roadside shieling after having diddled Davy Jones, a rainy night with a blind moon. Across the world for a wife. Quite a number of stories there were on that particular Alice Ben Bolt topic, Enoch Arden and Rip van Winkle and does anybody hereabouts remember Caoc O'Leary, a favourite and most trying declamation piece by the way of poor John Casey and a bit of perfect poetry in its own small way. Never about the runaway wife coming back, however much devoted to the absentee. The face at the window! Judge of his astonishment when he finally did breast the tape and the awful truth dawned upon him anent his better half, wrecked in his affections. You little expected me but I've come to stay and make a fresh start. There she sits, a grasswidow, at the selfsame fireside. Believes me dead, rocked in the cradle of the deep. And there sits uncle Chubb or Tomkin, as the case might be, the publican of the Crown and Anchor, in shirtsleeves,

eating rumpsteak and onions. No chair for father. Broo! The wind! Her brandnew arrival is on her knee, *postmortem child*. With a high ro! and a randy ro! and my galloping tearing tandy, O! Bow to the inevitable. Grin and bear it. I remain with much love your brokenhearted husband D. B. Murphy. (510–11)

There is an interesting discontinuity in the dynamics of this paragraph. It is like an illustration in a book to which the quotation in the caption does not correspond satisfactorily. That is, Bloom's introduction does not sit naturally with the wonderful monologue of the returned sailor; the passage certainly does not flow quite as smoothly from the ruminative to the comic as the two passages we saw in "Hades" and "Lestrygonians" did. The paragraph divides readily between Bloom's introduction of the theme and the comic monologue if the rhetorical imperative ("Judge of his astonishment") is seen as the caesura. The monologue is more fulllblown than either the "love vendetta" and the "domestic rumpus" on the one hand or the journalistic material from "Hades" and "Lestrygonians" on the other, but it still does not attain the stature of an interruption in "Cyclops" or a fantasy in "Circe." However, although the monologue is a magically self-contained little tableau,[6] the preamble is equally worthy of attention. The important thing to bear in mind is that the monologue is not supposed to be naturalistic, that it is an imitation of a fictional speech. Bloom's references to Enoch Arden and Rip van Winkle do prepare the way for this, and there is an old-fashioned novelistic tone in the rhetorical imperative immediately preceding the monologue.[7] The speech is such a vivid performance though that it dissolves the artificial boundaries that have been set out for it. I find myself savoring its domestic color and jovial irony and am thus unable to pass it off as either a casual sequence from Bloom's thoughts or another one of the narrator's erratic scenarios. Its brief poetic integrity is unique in this episode of circumlocution and obfuscation: it stands thus as a crucial reminder of the inventiveness that passed out of the novel when the vision of Rudy faded.

The tiredness of the language in "Eumaeus" should not be taken as a failure of authorial vision. What has happened is that the mistrust of words, no matter how artfully arranged they may be, that was a motivating factor for so many of the formal contortions from "Sirens" onward, has been brought to its logical conclusion in a chapter where even the ingenious Joycean linguistic structures have collapsed and we are left with the customary rubble not only of traditional prose fiction but of *Ulysses* as well. Thematically "Eumaeus" is impoverished, too: the meeting of Stephen and Bloom is an anticlimax, affirming only the evanescent nature of human communication. In the end it is treachery that pervades the chapter the way music pervades "Sirens," warping the very sentences themselves. After the nearly continuous explosion of the previous five episodes the words in "Eumaeus" float like so much charred debris that will not abide anywhere long. Of course Bloom's thoughts are crowded with examples of treachery, nowhere more so than when the cabbies discuss the Parnell story, at which point it becomes clear that the style itself dramatizes this preoccupation.[8]

The discussion of Parnell and Kitty O'Shea prompts Bloom to link the celebrated affair with his own pathetic lot. He produces a photograph of Molly and all but offers her to Stephen. These acts, largely acts of thought, form the vortex of the chapter around which all the images of betrayal swirl. As Bloom rehearses the great love story of recent Irish history in his mind and flogs the shock value out of the idea of adultery, the real insidiousness of the episode's linguistic failure becomes apparent. A protective covering of dead words can stop the ambivalent meanings of life from bristling problematically and any proposition, no matter how outrageous, can be domesticated in this way. So Bloom attempts to convince himself that adultery is unavoidable, since sexual love is, after all, the most natural thing in the world. This careening train of unreason brings us to the point at which Bloom finds himself involuntarily entertaining the notion of offering his wife to the young man. What is of interest to me is the part played by numbing verbal repetition in all this. Consider the two similar adulterous scenarios that cloud Bloom's perception when he thinks first of Parnell and Kitty O'Shea and then, as Stephen peruses the picture, of the consoling thought that adultery is perfectly ordinary.

> As regards Bloom he, without the faintest suspicion of a smile, merely gazed in the direction of the door and reflected upon the historic story which had aroused extraordinary interest at the time when the facts, to make matters worse, were made public with the usual affectionate letters that passed between them full of sweet nothings. First it was strictly Platonic till nature intervened and an attachment sprang up between them till bit by bit matters came to a climax and the matter become the talk of the town till the staggering blow came. (531)

> An awful lot of makebelieve went on about that sort of thing involving a lifelong slur with the usual splash page of gutterpress about the same old matrimonial tangle alleging misconduct with professional golfer or the newest stage favourite instead of being honest and aboveboard about the whole business. How they were fated to meet and an attachment sprang up between the two so that their names were coupled in the public eye was told in court with letters containing the habitual mushy and compromising expressions leaving no loophole to show that they openly cohabited two or three times a week at some wellknown seaside hotel and relations, when the thing ran its normal course, became in due course intimate. (534)

This emasculated language reminds us that sexual love is not only the most natural thing in the world but the oldest as well. These pictures emanate from the weak position of an excluded and envious onlooker: we recall the telling reference to "the other lucky mortal" in the "love vendetta." Bloom has been deliberately not thinking of this subject all day and now he stops restraining himself. In the passages above we see him submitting readily to that which is socially reassuring in the deflated repetition of newspaper stories.[9] There is a tremor of excitement in his consideration of Parnell's love, but he is more at home with the balanced resignation of the second account. This language is a far better instrument for reduction than it is for enlargement, as I will show in a moment when I look at the descriptions of Bloom's brief encounter with Parnell. In the descriptions of adultery here the outlook becomes more abstracted as Bloom frames the image that strikes him so painfully close to the bone. In both accounts we hear of attachments springing up, but in the second they merely run their normal course and become intimate instead of coming to a climax with a staggering blow as they did in the earlier version's comparatively racy language. A creeping cynicism has taken over from what was at least tolerance, if not endorsement, of human folly: so the reference to "the usual affectionate letters that passed between them full of sweet nothings" is recycled in a flattened form as "letters containing the habitual mushy and compromising expressions." The worn-out language is helpful then when it can be used as the dressing that makes something distasteful palatable. It cannot recreate the figure cut by Parnell on his last campaign, however. There are two versions of Bloom's brush with the great leader; one is an unspoken reflection, the other a copiously detailed anecdote. In an obvious bid to win Stephen's favor, Bloom expands his reminiscence to five times its original length. Like the two descriptions of adultery above and the husband-and-wife confrontations quoted earlier, the accounts of Bloom's meeting with Parnell form a juxtaposition that illuminates the anti-style of "Eumaeus."

He saw him once on the auspicious occasion when they broke up the type in the *Insuppressible* or was it *United Ireland,* a privilege he keenly appreciated, and, in point of fact, handed him his silk hat when it was knocked off and he said *Thank you,* excited as he undoubtedly was under his frigid exterior notwithstanding the little misadventure mentioned between the cup and the lip: what's bred in the bone. (531)

He, B, enjoyed the distinction of being close to Erin's uncrowned king in the flesh when the thing occurred on the historic fracas when the fallen leader's, who notoriously stuck to his guns to the last drop even when clothed in the mantle of adultery, (leader's) trusty henchmen to the number of ten or a dozen or possibly even more than that penetrated into the printing works of the *Insuppressible* or no it was *United Ireland* (a by no means by the by appropriate appellative) and broke up the typecases with hammers or something like that all on account of some scurrilous effusions from the facile pens of the O'Brienite scribes at the usual mudslinging occupation reflecting on the erstwhile tribune's private morals. Though palpably a radically altered man he was still a commanding figure though carelessly garbed as usual with that look of settled purpose which went a long way with the shillyshallyers till they discovered to their vast discomfiture that their idol had feet of clay after placing him upon a pedestal which she, however, was the first to perceive. As those were particularly hot times in the general hullaballoo Bloom sustained a minor injury from a nasty prod of some chap's elbow in the crowd that of course congregated lodging some place about the pit of the stomach, fortunately not of a grave character. His hat (Parnell's) a silk one was inadvertently knocked off and, as a matter of strict history, Bloom was the man who picked it up in the crush after witnessing the occurrence meaning to return it to him (and return it to him he did with the utmost celerity) who panting and hatless and whose thoughts were miles away from his hat at the time all the same being a gentleman born with a stake in the country he, as a matter of fact, having gone into it more for the kudos of the thing than anything else, what's bred in the bone instilled into him in infancy at his mother's knee in the shape of knowing what good form was came out at once because he turned round to the donor and thanked him with perfect *aplomb,* saying: *Thank you, sir,* though in a very different tone of voice from the ornament of the legal profession whose headgear Bloom also set to rights earlier in the day, history repeating itself with a difference, after the burial of a mutual friend when they had left him alone in his glory after the grim task of having committed his remains to the grave. (534–35)

The anecdote is colossally overdone and in its exaggerated dimensions we can see the operative mechanism of the episode's incompetent narrative. Both Bloom's loyalty to the deposed leader and his game attempt to impress this fact upon Stephen are touching. The root of the pathos lies in the latent but conspicuously undeveloped humor of Bloom's muddled attempt to characterize Parnell at the moment his hat is returned to him. The discrepancy between the incident and its labored presentation could have been broadly comic, but Joyce insures that it is not. Bloom's appearance as a spear-carrier in the drama of history is not to be laughed away, nor are his hours with Stephen. So with exquisite awkwardness the narrative registers Bloom's inability to muster the rhetorical force the moment calls for. All the attempts to lend moral authority to the tale through the descriptions of Parnell and his adversaries falter under their excessive adjectival and adverbial weight, an imbalance that mars three of the four sentences, Bloom's note about the elbow he received in the stomach being the sole exception. The closing reference to the snub from Menton at Paddy Dignam's funeral does have the appropriate ring of indignation, turning an afterthought into a quiet climax, but Bloom may only let slip this personal note when his companion's indifference leads him to suspect he is talking to himself. And yet the everyday decency of this last point corrects the scattershot quality in the moralizing about Parnell's struggle, returning Bloom's perception to the kind of wrongs a conventional middle-class novel can address. The magisterial Parnell throws the picture out of focus. The linguistic flotsam and jetsam is at last commensurate only with the awful smallness of the acts that give witness to Bloom's good faith, his gesture to Parnell and his concern for Stephen.

Some comfort may be drawn from the straightforward delivery of the silent version of Bloom's anecdote. Its humble honesty prevents the incipient clichés at the end ("the little misadventure mentioned between the cup and the lip: what's bred in the bone") from being a blemish; by contrast, the two phrases stitched onto the end of the homecoming sailor's monologue ("Bow to the inevitable. Grin and bear it") are a real betrayal of the lively material they follow. There is conviction behind the sparing use of the clichés in the sentence about Parnell emerging after the violent scene at the newspaper office. It should be noted, however, that this sentence is the only factual statement in a page of speculations about the possibility of Parnell's return.[10] Once again we are reminded that "Eumaeus" is a tissue of fiction on which the actions of the characters are incompletely imprinted. At the same time we must acknowledge the author's admission of the impossibility of ever setting down all that these two men might have thought or said on such a night. By constructing a narrative that looks like a piece of found prose, Joyce advertises his awareness of all the betrayals of the reality of experience a novelist commits every time he puts pen to paper.[11] We do have the detail of Murphy's preference for "good old Hollands and water" though, pointing furtively to the existence of an empirical basis for the episode, and we have the various adulterous scenarios that suggest the inexorable circling of Bloom's mind around the calamitous occurrence in his house. We even have a tantalizing clue to the nature of the strange pleasure we derive from all these crumpled equivocations in the description of Molly in "the slightly soiled photo creased by opulent curves" in which the slight soiling is "only an added charm like the case of linen slightly soiled" (533–34). In these ways Joyce asserts his desire to record what he can of the cabman's shelter in spite of the frailty of words and, in doing so, he offers us the half-truths that come between the dreaminess of "Circe" and the precision of "Ithaca."

8

The Fractured Realism of "Ithaca"

Joyce uses the catechism of "Ithaca" as a vehicle for exploring the limitations of prose fiction. As a homecoming to the factual world that has been obscured by the various styles in the latter half of *Ulysses,* the episode is acutely ambivalent. The exhaustive catechism does have a documentary value that is particularly satisfying after the equivocations of "Eumaeus." Our first reaction to the penultimate chapter, though, is a combination of gratitude for its apparent truthfulness and irritation at the polysyllabic unwieldiness of its scientific and legalistic language. Certainly readers negotiating *Ulysses* for the first time wonder if the anticlimactic conversation with Stephen and return to Molly could not have been delivered in simpler terms. Paradoxically, however, the events of "Ithaca," the episode that seems so pedantically objective, are inseparable from Joyce's prose representations of them; that is, the clinical language actually invests random details with a luminosity they would lack if they were presented more colloquially.[1] The episode's obsessively rational manner only serves to emphasize the homeliness beneath its intricate verbal surface. The encyclopedic answers dutifully remind us of "the incertitude of the void" (572), the "cold of interstellar space" (578) and "the apathy of the stars" (604), but our appreciation of the anecdotal and the incidental is enhanced by these vast and sobering perspectives. The juxtapositions of the domestic and the cosmic increase the stature of the domestic: for every sparkling reference to "the infinite lattiginous scintillating uncondensed milky way" (573), there are several hilarious incongruities like the description of Bloom's bellybutton as his "umbilicular fossicle" (584). The intermittent bursts of lyricism or insight are offset by longer stretches in which modest details are painstakingly recorded.

Perhaps the most dramatic example of this counterpoint occurs towards the end of the meeting with Stephen. The crucial pages immediately preceding Stephen's departure (568–76) are largely devoted to Bloom's thoughts of Milly and his disquisition on the stars. His reverie on Milly's funny ways occupies the silence after Stephen's tactless song about little Harry Hughes and the Jew's daughter, while the inventory of the galaxies is a final bid to impress the young man, so both themes arise from the inadequacies of the encounter. The descriptions of Milly gain from the proximity of the material about the "heaventree of stars hung with humid nightblue fruit" (573)[2] in much the same way as Bloom's interior monologue in "Sirens" gains from the image of Shakespeare that is transposed from the library scene (166, 230). The astronomical catalogues are tangential to the meditation on Milly, since it mentions Bloom's explanations of natural phenomena to her. In "Ithaca" such tangents are the closest equivalent we have to the burlesque, parody, pastiche and hallucination of previous episodes and, just as the meanderings of "Eumaeus" seem colorless after "Circe" and "Oxen of the Sun," so the Ithacan lists seem pedestrian; but "Eumaeus" and "Ithaca" are fascinating, not because of any flamboyance, but because they are attempts to mold a guarded, provisional realism in the aftermath of all the narrative experiments.[3] Chastened by the last few episodes, readers come to "Ithaca" with a keen sense of the frailty of language as a representational medium. So when we smile at the sketch of Milly's feline qualities, we are not just acknowledging her charm: cognizant of the perils of rendering anything in prose, we marvel at the author's ability to treat the joy of fatherhood without being maudlin. The verbal precision of "Ithaca" raises our awareness of the act of composing prose fiction to an unprecedented level. Reading the comparison of Milly and the cat, we are conscious of the pains taken to achieve a placid exactness and thoroughness.

In other respects were their differences similar?

In passivity, in economy, in the instinct of tradition, in unexpectedness.

As?

Inasmuch as leaning she sustained her blond hair for him to ribbon it for her (cf neckarching cat). Moreover, on the free surface of the lake in Stephen's green amid inverted reflections of trees her uncommented spit, describing concentric circles of waterrings, indicated by the constancy of its permanence the locus of a somnolent prostrate fish (cf mousewatching cat). Again, in order to remember the date, combatants, issue and consequences of a famous military engagement she pulled a plait of her hair (cf earwashing cat). Furthermore, silly Milly, she dreamed of having had an unspoken unremembered conversation with a horse whose name had been Joseph to whom (which) she had offered a tumblerful of lemonade which it (he) had appeared to have accepted (cf hearthdreaming cat). Hence, in passivity, in economy, in the instinct of tradition, in unexpectedness, their differences were similar. (569)

As an imitation of a scientific or legal document this description is imperfect: the traces of human feeling it bears are unmistakable. It is more like a journal entry made by a writer who has scrupulously checked his emotions because of the possibility of publication. The language yields a few indications of the spirit of paternal affection that orders the items in the list. This is not to say that Bloom is the author of "Ithaca" but just to note how fully Joyce has imagined the love of father for daughter. The regularity with which the compound participles charting the positions of the cat recur is itself amusing, as is the translation of Milly's innocent dream into the style of the catechism. The detail of the "tumblerful of lemonade" appears with ease amid the parenthesized confusion about whether or not the pronominal references to Joseph the horse should be impersonal. The plain image of the "waterrings" among the Latinate words and geometric details of the earlier sentence gives a similarly refreshing hint of fatherly wonder. The pleasure betrayed by such language goes beyond that of the ruminating character to that of the writer of the list. Something of Joyce's satisfaction with his attempt to enumerate dispassionately and accurately shows through.

The pretense of detachment seems almost transparent by the time we reach the last answer in the series dealing with Milly. Having been told how Bloom tries to impart his practical and scientific knowledge to her, the catechist asks:

In what manners did she reciprocate?

She remembered: on the 27th anniversary of his birth she presented to him a breakfast moustachecup of imitation Crown Derby porcelain ware. She provided: at quarter day or thereabouts if or when purchases had been made by him not for her she showed herself attentive to his necessities, anticipating his desires. She admired: a natural phenomenon having been explained by him to her she expressed the immediate desire to possess without gradual acquisition a fraction of his science, the moiety, the quarter, a thousandth part. (569–70)

This litany of praises gives Milly status approaching that of a mythic figure. We have passed from the endearing peculiarities of an ordinary girl to the solicitude of someone who is almost an ideal of filial piety. There is a suggestion, too, of what could be called poetic imagination behind the carefully pronounced tributes to her memory, her providence and her admiration, even though the examples illustrating these solemn declarations are marked by a fussiness about conjunctions ("by him not for her . . . by him to her") that is more in keeping with the catechist's usual manner. The final phrases of the answer allow us to hear strains of Milly's voice at its most breathlessly adoring, an attitude that is rare enough if we are to believe the censorious view of her that predominates in Molly's soliloquy.

It is important to bear in mind that the harmoniousness of the pictures of Milly is indicative not of any concord between Bloom and Stephen but of Bloom's absorption in his own thoughts. Further evidence of the distance between the two can be found a few pages later in the sequence of questions and answers dealing with the stars which, despite its impressive astronomical terminology, must also be read as an oblique summary of dialogue. Beneath the exalted catechism, the drama of failed communication continues out in the garden. The catechism's failure to reproduce exactly what was said is emblematic of the shortcomings of the encounter. It is possible to see the drift of the conversation in the longest of the astronomy answers as Bloom tries one last time to parade his knowledge only to be interrupted by his companion. About halfway through the answer, there is a clear movement away from the scientific and rational towards the literary and skeptical.[4] This movement is accompanied by a falling off in the power of the language. At first we are beguiled by a stream of exotic words.

> Which various features of the constellations were in turn considered?

> The various colours significant of various degrees of vitality (white, yellow, crimson, vermilion, cinnabar): their degrees of brilliancy: their magnitudes up to and including the 7th: their positions: the waggoner's star: Walsingham way: the chariot of David: the annular cinctures of Saturn: the condensation of spiral nebulae into suns: the interdependent synchronous discoveries of Galileo, Simon Marius, Piazzi, Le Verrier, Herschel, Galle: the systematisations attempted by Bode and Kepler of cubes of distances and squares of times of revolution: the almost infinite compressibility of hirsute comets and their vast elliptical egressive and reentrant orbits from perihelion to aphelion: the sidereal origin of meteoric stones: the Libyan floods on Mars about the period of the birth of the younger astroscopist: the annual recurrence of meteoric showers about the period of the feat of S. Lawrence (martyr, 10 August). . . . (574–75)

The appeal of the specialized language here is irresistible, so much so that the meeting of minds that was presented as an inspiring possibility in the De Quincey pastiche in "Oxen of the Sun" seems finally to be taking place.[5] I argued that the two consciousnesses appeared momentarily to blur in the hospital refectory, but now, as the examination of the firmament continues, the soaring language begins to wane in a dramatization of the evanescent nature of such possibilities.[6] The dissipation corresponds to the introduction of literary references.

> The monthly recurrence known as the new moon with the old moon in her arms: the posited influence of celestial on human bodies: the appearance of a star (1st magnitude) of exceeding brilliancy dominating by night and day (a new luminous sun generated by the collision and amalgamation in incandescence of two nonluminous exsuns) about the period of the birth of William Shakespeare over delta in the recumbent neversetting constellation of Cassiopeia and of a star (2nd magnitude) of similar origin but of lesser brilliancy which had appeared in and disappeared from the constellation of the Corona Septentrionalis about the period of the birth of Leopold Bloom and of other stars of (presumably) similar origin which had (effectively or presumably) appeared in and disappeared from the constellation of Andromeda about the period of the birth of Stephen Dedalus, and in and from the constellation of Auriga some years after the birth and death of Rudolph Bloom, junior, and in and from other constellations some years before or after the birth or death of other persons. . . . (575)

The pitch of the answer really has lowered considerably by this stage. At the beginning we could hear the awe of Bloom's commentary in limpid phrases like "annular cinctures" and "spiral nebulae," but now an ironic undertow can be felt.[7] Stephen's more cynical erudition underlines the diffuse nature of Bloom's knowledge and, by implication, of all the Ithacan catalogues. By casting an ironic light on "the posited influence of celestial on human bodies" Stephen's contribution to the dialogue emphasizes the tentativeness of this homecoming. The analogy between Bloom and Shakespeare and the paternal element in Bloom's relationship with Stephen are both finally called into question. The gradually lowering pitch of the massive sentence can be measured in the wry repetition of Bloom's terms "brilliancy" and "magnitude." The paragraph ends somberly with images of eclipse that add to the sense of disintegration: "the attendant phenomena of eclipses, solar and lunar, from immersion to emersion, abatement of wind, transit of shadow, taciturnity of winged creatures, emergence of nocturnal or crepuscular animals, persistence of infernal light, obscurity of terrestrial waters, pallor of human beings" (575).

As the two men look up into the cold night sky the text is momentarily enveloped in a profound gloom, which serves to remind us that Joyce's comedy, like the "mystical estate" of fatherhood in Stephen's Shakespeare lecture (170), is indeed founded upon "the incertitude of the void." The ironic intelligence associated with Stephen is a constituent force in the book. Bloom assents to Stephen's skepticism, admitting that the so-called heaventree is "a Utopia, there being no known method from the known to the unknown" (575). Nevertheless, as chilling as these thoughts are, they sharpen our perception of the humble integrity of Bloom's love for his daughter. Only a few small constants will mitigate Bloom's loneliness as he contemplates the "parallactic drift of socalled fixed stars" (573). The most fundamental of human bonds remains undiminished by the irony that so magisterially undercuts the notion of astrological influence. The vast breadth of "Ithaca" enables Joyce to dramatize the fragility of familial relationships without resorting to sentiment.

If *Ulysses* teaches us anything, it is that the dreams and idiosyncrasies of a Milly Bloom are as worthy of attention as the vagaries of the stars. And so her figure is imprinted on the firmament in the visionary De Quincey pastiche. In the world of Joyce's novel the stars are only important insofar as they illuminate the Blooms, the Dedaluses and all the other Dubliners,[8] and the pacified stylist of "Ithaca" can perform feats that rank with those of the pasticheur in "Oxen." Even the possibility of Shakespeare becoming Bloom by metempsychosis has not really been laid to rest: dismissed out in the garden, it is called forth again a few minutes later in the parlor when Bloom, overtaken by fatigue, is foreseen "reborn above delta in the constellation Cassiopeia . . . an estranged avenger, a wreaker of justice on malefactors" (598).[9] This particular mutation concludes the subdued catechistic equivalent of the hallucinatory trial scene and the messianic fantasy in "Circe," that is, the strange sequence that commences two pages earlier by reducing Bloom to the level of a "moribund lunatic pauper" (596).

The distortions of "Ithaca" are nevertheless only partially analogous to those of "Circe" or "Cyclops." Aside from the occasional droll touch there is an evenness, a deadpan quality, in the catechism's unrealistic tendencies. Where before there was the levity of parody and fantasy, we now have the gravity of hypothesis and conjecture.[10] The Ithacan interrogation does seize upon germs of figurative language that were only poetic intimations in the domain of the initial style, and turns them into flowerings of verbiage like those that blossom from the whims of burlesque and hallucination in "Cyclops" and "Circe." The book begins with Stephen musing that the theological evolution of the Roman Catholic Church is "like his own rare thoughts, a chemistry of stars" (17). Later, in a spasm of poetic inspiration on Sandymount strand, which foreshadows the reference to astronomy in his Shakespeare lecture (172), he thinks of his own form as a "darkness shining in brightness, delta of Cassiopeia" (40). Comparable intersections of the micro- and the macrocosm in "Cyclops" and "Circe" are cast in the motley trappings of parody and fantasy. We have the apparition of Paddy Dignam's "etheric double" with "orangefiery and scarlet rays emanating from the sacral regions and solar plexus" (247). In nighttown, a hobgoblin ushering in the end of the world and Elijah's second coming juggles tiny *"roulette planets"* that collide and are then transformed into helium-filled balloons (413). Joyce avails of the light-hearted modes of digression and fantasy to rehearse the imagery of transfiguration and apocalypse that will acquire a certain amount of seriousness when Bloom is presented as a heavenly body in "Ithaca." The catechism represents an intermediary style, more literal than the burlesques of "Cyclops" and "Circe" but partaking of a sporadic nocturnal wondrousness that is foreign to the initial style as well. No longer primarily concerned with the comic impulse that was behind many of the most bizarre distortions in "Cyclops" and "Circe," Joyce now confronts us with the nakedness of pure writing. Nowhere in *Ulysses* is the image of the mythic voyage treated with more poetic license than in the Ithacan answer that describes Bloom wandering "beyond the fixed stars and variable suns and telescopic planets, astronomical waifs and strays, to the extreme boundary of space, passing from land to land, among peoples, amid events" (598). The imaginative pitch is now such that the trappings of the occult are not needed to legitimate the cosmic flourish. I have noted how the language in the praises of Milly approaches the imaginative intensity of poetry and so threatens to transcend the level rationality of the catechism. Another feature that produces the same effect is the muting of the comic element that would have downplayed most attempts to portray Bloom as "an estranged avenger" or "a wreaker of justice on malefactors" in "Cyclops" or "Circe." In this respect the glamorous image of Bloom as a comet in the heavens resembles the description of his ascent at the end of "Cyclops," the evocations of the Elijah skiff in "Wandering Rocks" and even the vision of Rudy in "Circe."[11] So if the parodies and fantasies represent a kind of technicolor picture, the catechism is an immaculately developed black and white print.

Reading "Ithaca" is like going through the drawers of Bloom's table: we emerge with a sense not only of his foibles but of his dignity as well, having seen his erotic postcards and the documents that testify to his financial security. By the same token Joyce has deliberately woven flaws into his design; thus the catechism can be seen as a miscellany of offbeat descriptions, a medley that would be comparable to the sequence of interruptions in "Cyclops," except for the fact that in "Ithaca" the parodic element has been reduced to a vague but insistent undercurrent. For example, in the descriptions of Bloom's dream home and Molly's underwear, there is nothing of the brash comedy that fires the Cyclopean interruptions, and yet these catechistic responses are colored by seductive extraliterary stylizations. The description of the underwear is fetishistic, while that of the dream home reads like an advertisement.

So the strategic flaws of the catechistic narrative become especially apparent in the period between Stephen's departure and Bloom's return to Molly. It is during Bloom's brief vigil in the parlor that the curious emptiness behind the encyclopedic lucidity becomes noticeable. The episode's strict precision really is the counterpart of the less-grammatical inanity in "Eumaeus." The prose of "Eumaeus" draws upon the worn-out language of cliché, while the verbal materials of "Ithaca" are often extraliterary, and so the poetry of the chapter is necessarily as intermittent as that of its predecessor. It is true that the prose has been largely divested of the parodic element that was so prominent between "Sirens" and "Oxen of the Sun" and even, to a lesser extent, in "Circe," and this divestiture does lead to noble images like that of Bloom traversing the heavens; I cannot deny that the power of such moments is increased by the reader's boredom with some of the surrounding catechism, however. We rummage through "Ithaca," frustrated at certain times, inspired at others. For instance, when Bloom sits in his front room, smelling his toenail and taking stock of his life, I try to share in his thoughts of his dream home only to be rebuffed by the dismaying flatness of the prose. The description of the bungalow on the outskirts of Dublin (585–86) numbingly exemplifies the failure of the encyclopedic method, for it does not reproduce the peregrination of Bloom's mind and yet it is not unequivocally parodic either. It is just an extensive but banal list of domestic conveniences and paraphernalia. The banality emphasizes the lack of any ironic framework like that which Stephen supplies during the discussion of the stars.

The failure of the encyclopedic method, like the boredom it sometimes induces, is perfectly functional. We are now moving towards the disappearance of the last vestige of third-person narration in the episode's final dot and the subsequent advent of Molly Bloom. The impersonal vocabulary here will highlight the salty vigor of Molly's voice later. In the case of Bloom's bungalow the description actually bears some resemblance to the tableaux in the stage directions of "Circe." As the focus widens to include the property around the house and Bloom's activities there, the language takes on the mellow quality of a pastoral advertisement. Already, at the heart of the first description, there is a yearning for the security and repose that the word *home* connotes, a feeling that may escape our notice amid the masses of technical detail in the passage; it is there though in the root image of the whole catalogue: "a thatched bungalowshaped 2 storey dwellinghouse of southerly aspect . . . connected with the earth . . . rising, if possible, upon a gentle eminence with agreeable prospect . . . standing in 5 or 6 acres of its own ground, at such a distance from the nearest public thoroughfare as to render its houselights visible at night" (585).[12] The effect is like that of a real estate agent's well-phrased description of property. At the same time these almost neutral phrases suggest the setting of the scene in a traditional novel of rural life. In the words "if possible" I sense the conjectural quality that will color any citydweller's notion of a bucolic existence; by extension they might also be attributed to the urban novelist as he indulges the amusing whim of a pastoral vision. Only traces of Bloom's personality can be discerned in the heterogeneous list of household features and objects: the thermometer, the telephone, the "chronometer clock" and the "barometer with hydrographic chart" testify to his interests in science and technology. When we reach the reference to "mural paper at 10/- per dozen" (586) there is a hint that Bloom is inverting the nostalgia he felt in "Lestrygonians" for his early days with Molly and projecting his longing into an affluent future in which the value of his wallpaper is multiplied more than five times the "one and ninepence a dozen" he paid at Dockrell's for the paper in Lombard Street West (128). We remember too the "scenes truly rural of happiness of the better land with Dockrell's wallpaper at one and ninepence a dozen" (377) from Bloom's "long unintelligible speech" (376) in the Mary Driscoll case in "Circe." It is as difficult to follow the currents of Bloom's desire in the Flowerville vision as it is to perceive his unhappiness behind the summary of that speech in the stage directions of "Circe." The Bloom who will inhabit Flowerville is a far more contented figure than either the lonely husband of "Lestrygonians" or the hapless caricature who makes the "bogus statement" in response to Mary Driscoll's accusations (376). Now he assumes the role of the hero of the rural novel or the model in the pastoral advertisement.[13]

> Could Bloom of 7 Eccles street foresee Bloom of Flowerville?
>
> In loose allwool garments with Harris tweed cap, price 8/6, and useful garden boots with elastic gussets and wateringcan, planting aligned young firtrees, syringing, pruning, staking, sowing hayseed, trundling a weedladen wheelbarrow without excessive fatigue at sunset amid the scent of newmown hay, ameliorating the soil, multiplying wisdom, achieving longevity. (587)

Here is the Bloom who will become "resident magistrate or justice of the peace" (588). In case we fail to recognize our hero in these surroundings we are told that he will devote his spare time to the study of "folklore relative to various amatory and superstitious practices" and the "lecture of unexpurgated exotic erotic masterpieces" (587).

We must remember that we are reading a miniature fiction now, a narrative that bears an indeterminate relation to Bloom's thoughts of his finances and his ambition. Just as we could not be sure exactly how all the adulterous scenarios in "Eumaeus" related to Bloom's consciousness, so we cannot ascertain the fidelity of these descriptions to the "narrative concerning himself" (591) that Bloom habitually recounts before retiring. Presumably the vision of Flowerville represents Bloom's hopes with some accuracy: nevertheless the clinical approach of the catechism can be as artificial as the meanderings of "Eumaeus" or the parodies and pastiches in "Oxen of the Sun." The chief cause of my uncertainty about how to read the pastoral vision is the area of overlap between Joyce and Bloom as creators of the narrative; that is, when Bloom consoles himself in this way he obviously employs the skills he has acquired practicing what Professor MacHugh calls "the gentle art of advertisement" (111) and what he himself calls "the modern art of advertisement" (559). Bloom knows the prices of good wallpaper and Harris tweed caps. Joyce, too, has shown a familiarity with sums of money and rates of payment. In Stephen's parable, the savings and expenditures of the two women are recorded in detail (119), while in "Sirens" we are told how much the satin for the barmaids' blouses is worth (212). So advertising and naturalistic fiction draw upon similar materials, even though it would be as unsatisfactory to classify the Flowerville vision as simply an imitation of an advertisement as it would be to label "Aeolus" or "Sirens" as naturalistic fiction.[14] In "Aeolus," in "Sirens," and even in "Ithaca," the transcription of bald facts and figures is always offset by more playful and elaborate kinds of writing. Bloom's thoughts in the front room are firmly grounded in the world of money. He is wondering how to accumulate "vast wealth" (590) or at least avoid the "indignities" (596) or poverty. However, even as it exposes Bloom's hopes and fears, the catechism lays bare the novelist's artifice. The author's reluctance to issue conclusive documentation of the novel's climactic scenes is as evident here as it is in the patchwork effect of everchanging styles in "Oxen." The parodies and pastiches force us to imagine the dialogue in the hospital refectory for ourselves; similarly, the relentless questions and answers now prompt us to conduct our own inquiries into the facts of the book. The answers in the catechism, along with their accompanying questions, can be discrete units of verbiage like the individual imitations in "Oxen."

To return to the scene in the parlor then, we must surmise that the combination of the Wonderworker prospectus, the letter from Martha and Rudolph Bloom's suicide note diverts Bloom's mind from money, giving rise first to the memory of Rudolph's "migrations and settlements" (595) between Hungary and Ireland, and then to Bloom's own wanderlust (596–98). What he is really entertaining is the unlikely proposition of leaving his wife. Then the "cometary" wanderer and "estranged avenger" makes his ghostly, majestic appearance (598). The poetic drift of the text has departed from Bloom's sleepy meditations to lend the few steps to the bedroom the air of a mythic return.

The transformation of Bloom into a celestial body represents a bursting point in the catechism, an admission of the inadequacy of scientific, legalistic or commercial language in certain contexts. The momentary abandonment of any semblance of plausibility fulfills the promises of transcendence, implicit in the beguiling evocations of Milly and in the suggestion that Molly's window shines with supernatural splendor (576).[15] The apparition of the interplanetary Odysseus occurs just as it becomes clear that Bloom is about to join Molly in bed. We can now see that the descriptions of Bloom's dream home have the ring of weak advertising or inferior fiction because they are without the essential leavening agent of companionship, the presence of which would have enlarged the picture of Flowerville immeasurably. Of course, the reason Molly is so conspicuously absent from the Flowerville vision is that she is not simply a companion for Bloom: her individuality can no more be tailored to fit an advertisement or a well-made novel than Milly's can. The narrative innovation of the catechism, with its top-heavy lists, represents Joyce's refusal to engage in any such act of trimming. At the same time, the catechism's unwieldiness as a narrative tool signals the impossibility of recounting the events at 7 Eccles Street in a definitive fashion. In the context of such telling indirection it is appropriate that, instead of a reverential description of Molly herself, we are given a lovingly detailed account of her various items of discarded underwear. These are the first things Bloom sees when he comes into the room.

What miscellaneous effects of female personal wearing apparel were perceived by him?

A pair of new inodorous halfsilk black ladies' hose, a pair of new violet garters, a pair of outsize ladies' drawers of India mull, cut on generous lines, redolent of opoponax, jessamine and Muratti's Turkish cigarettes and containing a long bright steel safety pin, folded curvilinear, a camisole of batiste with thin lace border, an accordion underskirt of blue silk moirette, all these objects being disposed irregularly on the top of a rectangular trunk, quadruple battened, having capped corners, with multicoloured labels, initialled on its fore side in white lettering B. C. T. (Brian Cooper Tweedy). (600–601)

Joyce manages to make the catalogue as erotic as a verbal representation of lingerie without its human filling can be. The materials and the scents are named with the specificity that evidence of a miraculous occurrence or clues to an impossibly lascivious crime would merit. The glamour of such a list demonstrates how the prose of "Ithaca" sometimes threatens to combine the initial style's empiricism and the extravagance of the Cyclopean interruptions in a kind of fetishistic naturalism. At first the answer sounds like a simple list of purchases, but it develops into something like the text of an inspired advertisement in which exotic words are used to suggest faraway places.[16] The paternal devotion that colors the sketch of Milly earlier in the episode seems nebulous in comparison to the worshipful glow here. These are the precious commodities that might adorn a queen or a goddess, and perhaps also the "elegant courtesan, of corporal beauty, moderately mercenary, variously instructed, a lady by origin" with whom Bloom thinks of exercising his "virile power of fascination" after he has put Martha's letter in the drawer (594). After all, even Joyce's most celebratory language cannot annul the fact of Boylan's intrusion. Molly has not put on her finest silk and lace for Bloom today. The ironic implication of this catalogue of her undergarments may remind us of the clinical interlude in "Sirens" that foreshadows the Ithacan catechism, that is, the sentences informing us that Boylan wears a suit "made by George Robert Mesias, tailor and cutter, of number five Eden quay" and a straw hat "bought of John Plasto of number one Great Brunswick street, hatter" (229–30). Details of dress are enumerated with varying degrees of coolness as the usurper approaches and in the aftermath of his outrage. In the description of Molly's underwear, the catechism's extraordinary substantiality spills over into an erotic lyricism as ambivalent as Bloom's wounded love.

Often wonderfully lucid and occasionally overelaborated, the prose of "Ithaca" lies somewhere between the flowing realism of the initial style and the fantastic excess of the later parodic episodes. The catechism's language remains potent until the final dot marks the extinction of third-person narration in the book. In some ways the catechism represents the stylistic zenith of *Ulysses*: the discussion of the stars is sublime, even if it does hint at the gulf between Stephen and Bloom. Still, the facts about Milly, and the descriptions of the dream home and the underwear, are more characteristic of the prose in the episode as a whole. The light touch in the passages about Milly is indicative of the lack of finality in the catechism. On the other hand, Bloom's dream home and Molly's underwear are described with an excessive care that reminds us of the faint but unmistakable parodic strain in the episode. "Ithaca" proceeds by judicious indirections and, like the more flamboyantly unrealistic chapters before it, conveys truths that would otherwise have eluded us.

9

The Voice of "Penelope"

For readers who have been marvelling at the formal accomplishments of the previous eight episodes, the monologue of "Penelope" may seem anticlimactic, mere scribblings after acts of pure writing like "Oxen of the Sun" and "Ithaca." The question of style, or the pleasing lack of it, is relevant to Molly's soliloquy, however. The interesting thing is that, for the first time in *Ulysses,* Joyce has removed monologue from the decorative enclosure of third-person narration.[1] This is not a cosmetic adjustment: it means that the episode's sporadic poetry happens naturally as it might in the private sphere of letters or diary entries.[2] The avoidance of punctuation and conventional paragraphing is not a gimmick. Molly's soliloquy differs from the interior monologues of Bloom and Stephen in that her inaction, and the corresponding absence of an external narrator, produces an openness that has something of the madly inclusive Cyclopean catalogues or Circean hallucinations about it. In this way Molly's monologue is a private colloquial equivalent of the written public discourses of "Eumaeus" and "Ithaca." There is a sense in which Molly can say anything, just as anything can be assimilated into the numbing manners of the previous two episodes. Before the homecoming chapters this freedom only seemed to be presented in the neutralized modes of parody or fantasy. To a greater degree than either Stephen or Bloom, Molly can make fantasy reality, as the liaison with Boylan demonstrates. Her apparent ability to make things happen gives her whims a credibility and her lyricism an immediacy that we do not find in either the spectacular outpourings of "Cyclops" and "Circe" or the poetry of her husband's meditations.[3]

So Molly is as powerful as any of the narrators in *Ulysses.* It does not diminish her importance as a naturalistic character to say that her girlish volubility provides Joyce with an ideal discourse for the last episode of his book.[4] The medium of her imagination is used to present scenarios that, in a different context, would have acquired a tinge of parody. In other words, the flights of fancy in Molly's unpunctuated babble are far less stylized than, for example, the carefully constructed hallucinations in "Circe." The "cracked" ideas that come into Molly's head are at least possible, if not probable. Her consideration of the range of possibilities Stephen's presence would have afforded is a case in point.

Id have to introduce myself not knowing me from Adam very funny wouldnt it Im his wife or pretend we were in Spain with him half awake without a Gods notion where he is dos huevos estrellados senor Lord the cracked things come into my head sometimes itd be great fun supposing he stayed with us why not . . . Id love to have a long talk with an intelligent welleducated person Id have to get a nice pair of red slippers like those Turks with the fez used to sell or yellow and a nice semitransparent morning gown that I badly want or a peachblossom dressing jacket like the one long ago in Walpoles only 8/6 or 18/6 (641)

We expect Molly to be the Mediterranean beauty and here she slips guilelessly into the role. She also reinforces the dream image Bloom recollected in "Nausicaa" of her looking Turkish in red slippers and breeches (311–12). It is worth comparing Molly's vision of spontaneous play-acting here to the part she is assigned as *"a handsome woman in Turkish costume"* in Circe's drama. This set piece is drawn, to a certain extent, from Bloom's imagination and from the previous night's dream. It is rendered in the third-person narrative of the stage directions.

A VOICE

(*sharply*) Poldy!

BLOOM

Who? (*he ducks and wards off a blow clumsily*) At your service.

(*He looks up. Beside her mirage of datepalms a handsome woman in Turkish costume stands before him. Opulent curves fill out her scarlet trousers and jacket, slashed with gold. A wide yellow cummerbund girdles her. A white yashmak, violet in the night, covers her face, leaving free only her large dark eyes and raven hair.*) (358–59)

Several elements in this picture come from Bloom's interior monologue. As well as the dream image from "Nausicaa" there is the thought of Molly with the sheet up to her dark Spanish eyes that occurs to him in Sweny's shop (69). We may also detect a trace of the daydream about the East he has on the way to the porkbutcher's, in which he associates the violet of the strange night sky with Molly's new garters (47). Clearly the gloss of the stage direction comes from the snippets of pastiche and parody it contains, though: the *"opulent curves"* are of course familiar to us from *Sweets of Sin* (194) and the *"raven hair"* recalls the Cyclopean praises of "the ravenhaired daughter of Tweedy" (262). By introducing material from beyond the domain of the interior monologue, and especially by drawing in the epithet from a Cyclopean interruption, such embroiderings remind us that the fund of information in the book is greater than the contents of Bloom's mind or the minds of the three main characters put together. There is something clinical about the way the narrator of "Circe" sifts through these ingredients. In "Penelope" correspondences are not developed with such verbal precision. In fact Molly's vocabulary is so limited that it is surprising to find her repeating a polysyllable from the Ithacan catechism when she thinks of a corset advertisement that refers to "obviating that unsightly broad appearance across the lower back" (618), thus echoing "the necessity for repose, obviating movement" and "the proximity of an occupied bed, obviating research" which were among the reasons given for the wanderer's inertia a few minutes earlier (599). So, even though Molly's thoughts about what she might do with Stephen are as far removed from the plane of naturalistic verisimilitude and as close to the realm of fantasy as the paragraph from "Circe" here is, they do nevertheless have a quirky human believability that is not evident in the serene artificiality of the stage direction. Even Molly's Spanish phrases seem much more natural than, say, the Hebrew recited by Zoe Higgins in nighttown (389). We can only conclude that something like the scene Molly imagines might have taken place had Stephen stayed the night. The contrasting treatments of the dream image from "Nausicaa" in "Circe" and "Penelope" demonstrate how the final episode's monologue restores a sense of wonder to a motif that at first could only be revived within a neutral and implicitly ironic context.

As a narrator Molly's most formidable trait is her self-sufficiency. The appearance of artlessness is more important here than it has been in any other episode. For Penelope's lyricism to have the desired impact the reader must get the impression that finding the right word, or even finding comically inappropriate words, matters less now to Joyce. Molly's voice really does move beyond not only ornamental or figurative language but the mocking transcription of such language as well. In fact, just as her effusions occasionally equal the copious descriptions of "Circe," at their finest they also represent a plainspoken alternative to the poetry of the initial style. For example, if we compare Bloom's picture of Dublin bay from Howth head on the day of his proposal to the evocation of the view from Gibraltar on the morning Mulvey's ship went out, we can see that Penelope's less elegant prose has certain homespun virtues. The difference between the two presentations should be noted, however, for it shows how much narrative craft Joyce has set aside in order to surrender to the rhythm of "Penelope."[5] The tone of Bloom's interior monologue in Davy Byrne's is measured, guided by the hand of the third-person narrator. "Glowing wine on his palate lingered swallowed. Crushing in the winepress grapes of Burgundy. Sun's heat it is. Seems to a secret touch telling me memory. Touched his sense moistened remembered. Hidden under wild ferns on Howth below us bay sleeping: sky. No sound. The sky. The bay purple by the Lion's head. Green by Drumleck. Yellowgreen towards Sutton. Fields of undersea, the lines faint brown in grass, buried cities" (114). Molly's remembrance is more straightforwardly circumstantial. "I went up Windmill hill to the flats that Sunday morning with captain Rubios that was dead spyglass like the sentry had he said hed have one or two from on board I wore that frock from the B Marche paris and the coral necklace the straits shining I could see over to Morocco almost the bay of Tangier white and the Atlas mountain with snow on it and the straits like a river so clear" (627).

The movement from third-person narration to interior monologue in the "Lestrygonians" passage reflects a subtle psychological awakening. Molly just states where she went, what she wore and what she could see. The quotation from "Penelope" could be divided, roughly speaking, into three declarations, each beginning with the first person singular. Even the third-person narration in the "Lestrygonians" passage is less forceful that this, sketching the passive frame of Bloom's mind with participles until the interior monologue paints the landscape without having recourse to verbs at all. Both passages present vistas, although the annotations of Gifford and Seidman inform us that Molly could not possibly have seen either the bay of Tangier or the Atlas mountain.[6] Even so, the absence of third-person narration in "Penelope" ensures that the effect of these exotic names here is not blatantly artificial like the effect of the reference to "opoponax" and "jessamine" in "Ithaca" (600) or the reference to "the gardens of Alameda" in "Cyclops" (262).[7] The poetic potential of such material was suggested with varying degrees of emphasis in the embellishments of "Cyclops" and "Ithaca," but in the context of Molly's soliloquy it is brought to fruition. Molly's own treatment of her Mediterranean background lacks the ironic reverberations that accompany references to it in the more impersonal narrations.

It is in the fourth and fifth sentences of the soliloquy, when Molly remembers her friendship with Hester Stanhope and her dalliance with Mulvey, that the most sustained poetic evocations of Gibraltar occur. The two sentences are punctuated by the wailing of the train whistles Molly hears.[8] On this plaintive note her life in Dublin recedes and the lyricism of her distant past engulfs the text. This is achieved without ostentatious artifice. Unlike the oceanic yearning that emanates from the barmaids in the Ormond or the Eastern aroma that Zoe Higgins exudes, Molly's Gibraltar life is not imposed by way of metaphorical stratagems but exposed through a dramatic confession. Penelope's utterances are not governed by the same ideal of fine writing as the felicitous metaphors of "Sirens" and "Circe." One purpose of the echoing musical prose in "Sirens" is to offset metaphors that are a little too sumptuously melancholy: we are told, for example, that Miss Douce and Miss Kennedy "cowered under their reef of counter" (212) and later that they "pined in depth of ocean shadow" (221). And of course we remember the way the stage directions of "Circe" luxuriate in Zoe's corruption as she administers *"the passtouch of secret monitor"* and gives off *"the lion reek of all the male brutes that have possessed her"* (409). In "Penelope" the distance between narrator and event that allows such figurative language to flower has been abolished.[9] And yet the very absence of the mediating machinery of an omniscient or impersonal narrative lends Molly's voice poetic power as she remembers the incidents of her adolescence. The memories of Hester and Mulvey tend to flow side by side, mingling childlike playfulness with incipient sexuality. The admixture is apparent when she recalls the moment of her greatest intimacy with Hester: "we were like cousins what age was I then the night of the storm I slept in her bed she had her arms around me then we were fighting in the morning with the pillow what fun he was watching me whenever he got an opportunity at the band on the Alameda esplanade when I was with father and captain Groves" (622).

The appearance of the preying male does not cast too long a shadow over the girlish idyll. Molly's initiation seems to have been as uncomplicated as her language is now. We can imagine how Bloom's hallucinatory accusers in nighttown would have exploited a homoerotic encounter like the one with Hester on "the night of the storm." But the differences between "Penelope" and earlier episodes are not just a matter of character or the adaptation of language to character. The unpunctuated monologue, with its avoidance of third-person narration and metaphor, represents Joyce's emancipation from the rational habits of parody and irony that would surely have enervated any attempt to set Molly's thoughts in a more conventional fictional structure.[10] "Penelope" is the fulfillment of the evanescent promise of transcendence contained in paragraphs like the Cyclopean paean to the "chaste spouse of Leopold . . . Marion of the bountiful bosoms" (262) in which the effect of the artificial style on the subject is not wholly reductive. The parodic manner in which "the ravenhaired daughter of Tweedy" is described in the "gardens of Alameda" does not mask the fact that, just like all Bloom's fond musings upon his wife's "unique birthplace" (597), such a digression prepares us for the Gibraltar segments of "Penelope."

In fact, since descriptions like the paragraph in "Cyclops" or the stage direction quoted from "Circe" only do partial justice to Bloom's pride in her Mediterranean background, Molly herself must substantiate it. The voice of "Penelope" restores the lyricism of the initial style, which has been cheapened by the mocking narrator of *Ulysses* in his various guises. At the same time the soliloquy incorporates the sweep of the book's parodic tendency and thus enlarges the restored details. For example, at the end of "Nausicaa," when Bloom thinks movingly of Molly's girlhood in Gibraltar, the images he considers nearly all recur in connection with Mulvey in the fourth and fifth sentences of "Penelope." Although Bloom seems not to be concerned with Mulvey but with the romantic setting of Gibraltar, the specifics he recalls are used again by Molly in her account of the affair. The passage in "Nausicaa" is an act of imagination based on what Molly has told him about her youth. He has been thinking of the onset of Milly's puberty. "Poor child! Strange moment for the mother too. Brings back her girlhood. Gibraltar. Looking from Buena Vista. O'Hara's tower. The seabirds screaming. Old Barbary ape that gobbled all his family. Sundown, gunfire for the men to cross the lines. Looking out over the sea she told me. Evening like this, but clear, no clouds. I always thought I'd marry a rich gentleman coming with a private yacht. *Buenas noches, senorita. El hombre ama la muchacha hermosa.* Why me? Because you were so foreign from the others" (311).

The word "Gibraltar" obviously sets Bloom's mind alight, but these elegiac final pages of "Nausicaa" do not approach the quality of the book's dizzying last page the way the fourth and fifth sentences of Molly's soliloquy do. Bloom's meditation is awed and self-effacing. If Molly is awed it is by the thrill of her own escapades coming back to her in a torrent of memories. And she is anything but self-effacing. Just as her notions of forming a relationship with Stephen serve to inject mythopoeic power into the dream Bloom recollected in "Nausicaa," her account of the affair with Mulvey fleshes out Bloom's secondhand images of Gibraltar. Her only verbatim repetition of her husband's interior monologue ("gunfire for the men to cross the lines") occurs amid a wealth of atmospheric detail as she remembers the lull in garrison life between Hester's departure and the advent of Mulvey: "unfortunate poor devils of soldiers walking about with messtins smelling the place more than the old longbearded jews in their jellibees and levites assembly and sound clear and gunfire for the men to cross the lines and the warden marching with his keys to lock the gates and the bagpipes and only captain Groves and father talking about Rorkes drift and Plevna and sir Garnet Wolseley and Gordon at Khartoum" (623).[11]

It is clear that the brief lines in "Nausicaa" are only a sketch for the spacious canvas of "Penelope." In the fifth sentence, most of which is given over to her experiences with Mulvey,[12] Molly mentions O'Hara's tower, Barbary apes and screaming birds as she recalls her jubilation at being the object of his affections.

> Im always like that in spring Id like a new fellow every year up on the tiptop under the rockgun near OHaras tower I told him it was struck by lightning and all about the old Barbary apes they sent to Clapham without a tail careering all over the show on each others back (625)

> I was a bit wild after when I blew out the old bag the biscuits were in from Benady Bros and exploded it Lord what a bang all the woodcocks and pigeons screaming coming back the same way that we went over middle hill round by the old guardhouse (626)

Obviously Molly does more than fill in the lacunae in Bloom's interior monologue, although the progression from the evocative hearsay that makes up his picture of Gibraltar to the whole story straight from the horse's mouth is significant. Nor is it just a matter of Joyce allowing the woman his hero loves to speak: "Penelope" is the ultimate alternative to the initial style, the human babble that carries on when all the edifices of rhetoric and vocabulary have collapsed and been swept away. In Molly's unaffected idiom the Gibraltar material acquires a credibility that the earlier styles could not bestow upon it.

The opulent digressions, hallucinations and inventories of "Cyclops," "Circe" and "Ithaca" register the uniqueness of Molly's origins without quite capturing their romance as it is captured in the more modest discourse of "Penelope." The manifestation of this failure in "Cyclops" is interesting, because the digression about Molly parodies a kind of bardic literature. "Pride of Calpe's rocky mount, the ravenhaired daughter of Tweedy. There grew she to peerless beauty where loquat and almond scent the air. The gardens of Almeda knew her step: the garths of olives knew and bowed. The chaste spouse of Leopold is she: Marion of the bountiful bosoms'' (262).

As I noted in my discussion of ''Cyclops,'' there is an element of homage in the parody here,[13] especially in the middle two sentences where the particulars of setting are dispensed with a readiness that, however mannered, does approach the effortless flow of detail in ''Penelope.'' The lyrical resonance of Gibraltar is not entirely muted by the archaic diction. The unusual words here (''loquat,'' ''garths'') almost give dignity to the hackneyed phrases (''peerless beauty . . . chaste spouse''). A stalemate is reached between poetry and cliché, whereas in Molly's description of the morning of Mulvey's departure the imagery (''the coral necklace the straits shining'') is so radiant that we can overlook flaws like the geographical inaccuracies. Still, given the wayward spirit of the Cyclopean interruptions, it is possible to imagine the digression about Gibraltar blossoming into a list as heterogeneous as the one quoted above in which Molly records the military trappings and multiracial ambience of the garrison (623). Also, if we compare the digression's absence of metaphor to the figurative embroiderings of Zoe Higgins in ''Circe,'' we can see how the comic offhandedness of the pseudo-poetic clichés is liberating and, in that way, represents a step towards the babble of ''Penelope.'' However, the abandonment of self-conscious narration in favor of unfettered monologue for the definitive treatment of Gibraltar means that all traces of the archness, the pokerfaced detachment, that went with that self-consciousness are wiped away. In its place we get eight gigantic sentences, human ramblings that nevertheless, as Joyce told Budgen, turn ''like the huge earth ball slowly surely and evenly round and round spinning.''[14] In Molly's reminiscences of Gibraltar the sense of poetic utterance that was only hinted at in the portentously bardic Cyclopean digression is fully developed.

The operation of Molly's lyricism is particularly telling when she transfers the quality of her Mediterranean past to her hazy notion of what Stephen must be like. For Molly, after all, Stephen is a figure from long ago, someone who, like Hester, is to be seen ''all through a mist'' (622).[15] With virtually no empirical data to hinder her she is able to take the image of the ''darling little fellow in his lord Fauntleroy suit'' and recast it, just as Bloom recasts the image of Rudy at the end of ''Circe.'' But the vision of Rudy dramatizes Bloom's forlornness: Molly's thought of singing ''In Old Madrid'' to the budding poet reveals her simple spirit.

> they all write about some woman in their poetry well I suppose he wont find many like me where softly sighs of love the light guitar where poetry is in the air the blue sea and the moon shining so beautifully coming back on the nightboat from Tarifa the lighthouse at Europa point the guitar that fellow played was so expressive will I ever go back there again all new faces two glancing eyes a lattice hid Ill sing that for him theyre my eyes if hes anything of a poet

two eyes as darkly bright as loves own star arent those beautiful words as loves young star itll be a change Lord knows to have an intelligent person to talk to about yourself not always listening to him (637–38)

The restraints that applied when the title of this song crossed Bloom's mind in "Sirens" (226) have been lifted. The size of Molly's lilting quotation is indicative not only of her mastery of the song but also of her sovereignty over the narration. The replacement of figurative language with this kind of allusion signals the author's enraptured acquiescence to her nostalgic yearning, a position that makes the poignant record of Bloom's response to "M'Appari" seem impassive by comparison. Consequently Molly's imagination races helterskelter to the improbable leap in which Stephen is likened to Bloom's statue of Narcissus, a figure with whom even oral sex would be hygienic. The mechanism of fantasy can be seen coming subtly into play here as she matches the generous quotation from "In Old Madrid" with yet another incandescent memory of Gibraltar. As the soliloquy moves towards its climax it becomes clear that the idea of Stephen the "handsome young poet" (638) is her response to the wistful question "will I ever go back there again." In a few moments she will be associating the Latin sound of Dedalus with the names in Gibraltar and thinking how she can impress him with her Spanish (640–41). Molly may be foolish to think that Stephen would be interested in listening to her talk about herself, but such idle fancy does nevertheless testify to the self-assurance that animates her imagination and is so much rarer in her husband's meditations.

The wholesale quotation from the song shows how the lyricism of "Penelope" is evolved from a discourse which, like the clichés of "Eumaeus" and the legalese of "Ithaca," is potentially formless. Obviously the succession of interior monologues in the book from Stephen to Bloom to Molly represents a stripping away of layers of sophistication; what is less obvious is that the open form of Molly's soliloquy incorporates something of the extravagance we encountered in all the episodes from "Sirens" onward.[16] The rough and tumble speed of Molly's monologue just does not allow for the carefully assembled detail that characterizes, for example, Bloom's vision of the East on the way to the pork-butcher's (47). But then again it is only the shoals of clichés in "Eumaeus" or the polysyllabic flowerings of "Ithaca" that approach Molly's unpunctuated stream of reflections, since in both of those episodes Joyce strives to abdicate the instruments of fictional artifice. I have compared Molly's imagined Stephen to Bloom's vision of Rudy, but the last stage directions of "Circe" clinically enumerate the items of the fairy boy's costume in prose that is as sculpted as that of the Pater pastiche in "Oxen of the Sun" (344)[17] while, as I have shown, Molly's picture of Stephen consists of a series of notional scenarios colloquially expressed. The deadpan styles of "Eumaeus" and "Ithaca" blurred the division between realistic events and parody or hallucination that had been established in "Cyclops" and "Circe." In "Penelope," where we have monologue without a third-person narrative framework, there is no question of such a division. No narrative machinery is needed to deal with flights of fancy, as the ease with which Molly weaves a dream image of her own to accompany the lilting of "In Old Madrid" proves so magisterially.

Conclusion

The aim of this study has been to take the narrative strategies of *Ulysses* on their own terms. I have shown that the various styles only appear to hinder the story. In fact the techniques are expedients devised to reflect the comic incompleteness of the relationships between Bloom, Stephen and Molly. By imitating a miscellany of discourses that are more public and anonymous than the interior monologue and its accompanying narrator, Joyce gives his novel mythic and psychological breadth. I have emphasized the discourses of the last nine episodes then, allotting a chapter each to the longest and densest of them.

I have traced three broad developments of the styles of *Ulysses*: the transition from the initial style to the parodic techniques, the adaptation of these techniques for poetic purposes in "Oxen of the Sun" and "Circe," and the return to a qualified realism in the homecoming episodes. As I demonstrated in my two opening chapters, a restless, serendipitous spirit animates the first nine episodes of the book. The later forays into the colorful subliterary worlds of journalism, bad fiction, mannered essays, theatrical scripts and scientific or legal documents develop upon the wayward eclecticism of the interior monologue and its mutable narrative enclosure. The movement from interior monologue and realistic narration to parody, pastiche and fantasy is not as arbitrary as it seems. After all, the formidable allusiveness of Stephen's consciousness and the masses of fragmented quotations in Bloom's do prepare us for the later episodes, which occasionally resemble anonymous pieces of found prose. As Linda Hutcheon has pointed out, an ironic or critical intelligence can turn quotation and allusion into acts of parody.[1] Such transformations play a crucial role in the overall textual economy of the book. Furthermore, the associative principle of the interior monologue gains ascendancy over the whole narrative in "Wandering Rocks," and the vignettes of that episode in turn establish a formal precedent for the series of interruptions in "Cyclops" and the patchwork of stylistic imitations in "Oxen of the Sun." Even the verbal explosion in the stage directions and dialogue of "Circe" derives in part from an expansion of the associative, colloquial and dramatic properties of the interior monologue.

"Oxen of the Sun" is a watershed in that it demonstrates Joyce's total unwillingness to observe the decorum a fixed narrator would call for. The impact of this performance causes the last four episodes of the book to reverberate with indeterminacy. "Circe," "Eumaeus," "Ithaca" and "Penelope" all feature a plainer sense of representation than the narratives of "Sirens," "Cyclops," "Nausicaa" and "Oxen," and yet none of these final episodes really reproduces the straightforward clarity of the initial style. In the two-tiered dramatic structure of "Circe" we have, as John Paul Riquelme says, "the ghost of the initial style."[2] And of course "Eumaeus," "Ithaca" and "Penelope" only seem like repudiations of stylistic indulgence, since they contain flourishes like the vision of D. B. Murphy's homecoming (510–11), the luminous description of Bloom's astral wanderings (598), and Molly's fantasies about seducing Stephen (637–38, 641), all of which induce a sense of the relativism of narrative truth.

Considering the leveling effect of sleep and dreams in *Finnegans Wake,* Richard Ellmann has written: "By day we attempt originality; by night plagiarism is forced upon us."[3] Although I have not traced the roots of the *Wake* in the later episodes of *Ulysses,* many of the passages from the nighttime scenes that I have analyzed do approach the kind of revelatory borrowing or appropriation Ellmann suggests.[4] The descent into the subliterary was a creative boon for Joyce. By producing parodies of journalistic or novelistic writing, pastiches of English prose styles and imitations of stage directions and a catechism, he was able to explore the kinship between lies and myths, human and linguistic treachery. Behind all the performances there is a perception of the ways the verbal flotsam and jetsam of popular culture affects our emotional lives. Karen Lawrence argues that the writing in "Circe" shows how "in the unconscious, myth and melodrama, archetype and stereotype merge."[5] The imitations of public discourses are strategically flawed forgeries that direct us to the overlapping areas Lawrence identifies.

The basic premise of this study has been that the obliqueness of the later episodes is in itself meaningful, that the qualities dramatized by the various styles could not have been dramatized in any other way. I have looked at passages in which judicious indirections are employed to express truths that could not have been as successfully rendered in the initial style. It is not that the material involved in such passages is too lofty for the interior monologue and its accompanying narrator: in fact many of them deal with a species of disappointment or absence. None of them is entirely about what it purports to be about: the obtrusive narrative methods constantly reveal aspects of the novel's great anticlimax, its mythic and psychological groundswell.

Every reader of *Ulysses* knows that something happens during the afternoon episodes and that the book is never the same again. This study has been an account of what happens to Joyce's prose after the disappearance of the initial style. I have contended that the parodies, pastiches, stage directions and catechism represent public discourses through which the drama of Bloom, Stephen and Molly is filtered. It is clear also that the anticlimactic shape of the story is boldly delineated by a series of stylistic climaxes that includes "Oxen of the Sun," "Circe," and parts of "Ithaca" and "Penelope." But Joyce is not using verbal fireworks to distract us from the paucity of action in his novel. The styles cast light upon certain areas of human emptiness and they do so, as John Henry Raleigh has noted, by satirizing "modern journalism" and varieties of "decorous middle-class Victorian rhetoric."[6] That is, Joyce appropriates the idioms of newspapers and popular fiction, to name just two of his sources, in order to show the sorts of things they exclude. This process is not undertaken solely as an attack on such forms of writing: Joyce is obviously captivated by the aesthetic opportunities these corrupt discourses afford. Indeed the purpose of this study has been to persuade readers that the last nine episodes of *Ulysses* represent not just a compendium of parodies and literary experiments but a record of fugitive emotions, too. The summary of Bloom's speech from the dock in "Circe" attains a kind of poetry, as does the account of Gerty MacDowell's world in the first part of "Nausicaa." Joyce's comic genius works against the clichés and figurative language he employs, highlighting its intricate inappropriateness and suggesting recesses of feeling that would usually lie outside its range.

The homecoming episodes, "Eumaeus" and "Ithaca," bring a realism that is nevertheless distorted by the use of cliché and catechism. In fact, what has happened is that Joyce has blurred the distinction between his parodic and realistic techniques and absolved himself of the obligation to choose between being funny or straight-faced. The line separating action from digression, or realism from distortion, is abolished and we recognize the frailty of fictional narrative itself. Still, there is something liberating in this recognition, because the styles of *Ulysses* ultimately bear witness to the integrity of the novel's human story. So we sift through the rubble of clichés in "Eumaeus" and the mountains of information in "Ithaca," amazed by the possibilities for communication that remain in the scorched language.[7] "Penelope" represents a final yoking together of the colloquial, confessional spirit of the interior monologue and the virtuosity of the more poetic alternatives to the initial style. In this transcendent development of a less public discourse that resembles a diary or an epistolary effusion, Joyce cultivates the lyricism which was neutralized in the copious figurative language of "Cyclops" and "Circe," thus magisterially vindicating the search for new styles in the afternoon and evening episodes.

To say that *Ulysses* meanders off into arid stylistic experimentation after the first two hundred pages would be to do Joyce a disservice. We are still learning to read the last two-thirds of this book. Each of the styles is perfectly right in its own way and together they make up a gallery of Joycean masks. In fact it is only common sense to see the author of *Finnegans Wake* gradually emerging through the last nine episodes of *Ulysses*. However, it was not the purpose of this study to trace that evolution in terms of the *Wake*. What I have tried to do is characterize the various stages in the book's inexorable drift away from realism.

Ultimately this has meant an examination of each piece of writing on its own terms as well as a sense of the whole formed by the eighteen episodes. In attempting to set down my sense of each episode's shape and texture, I hope I have filled in a few lacunae in the existing commentaries. I hope also that my investigation of the counterpoints established by the various styles remains true to the spirit of *Ulysses*, the Joycean spirit that challenges us to question all our assumptions about reading and writing.

Notes

Introduction

1. In his provocative book, *Resisting Novels: Ideology and Fiction,* Lennard J. Davis slights Joyce for never questioning the validity of the authorial enterprise the way Sterne does in *Tristram Shandy.* Such criticism overlooks the absolute necessity of the author's intrusive role in *Ulysses.* Davis, *Resisting Novels: Ideology and Fiction* (London: Metheun, 1987), pp. 157–58.

2. Harry Levin, *James Joyce* (Norfolk, Conn.: New Directions, 1941), p. 106.

3. Richard Ellmann, *James Joyce* (New York and London: Oxford University Press, 1959), pp. 367–68.

4. Ibid., p. 370.

5. Linda Hutcheon, *A Theory of Parody: The Teachings of Twentieth-Century Art Forms* (London: Methuen, 1985).

6. Richard Ellmann, *Ulysses on the Liffey* (New York: Oxford University Press, 1972), p. 135.

7. Hayman writes: "I use the term 'arranger' to designate a figure who can be identified neither with the author nor with his narrators, but who exercises an increasing degree of overt control over his increasingly challenging materials." The best guide to Joyce's intricate verbal cross-referencing is still Hanley's *Word Index*. David Hayman, *"Ulysses": The Mechanics of Meaning* (Englewood Cliffs, N.J.: Prentice-Hall, 1970), p. 70; Miles L. Hanley, *Word Index to James Joyce's "Ulysses"* (Madison: University of Wisconsin Press, 1937).

8. In "Lestrygonians" Bloom imagines the statues of goddesses "drinking electricity" and addressing him as "Mortal"; in "Circe" the Nymph does call him "Mortal" and brags of eating "electric light" (144, 444, 449).

9. In Tennyson's poem Ulysses says, "I will drink / Life to the lees."

10. French interprets these sentences as a warning to readers that the point of view will shift in "Scylla and Charybdis" and a preview of the mocking voices of "Sirens" and "Cyclops." Marilyn French, *The Book as World: James Joyce's "Ulysses"* (Cambridge, Mass.: Harvard University Press, 1976), pp. 108–9.

11. Richard Ellmann, ed., *Selected Letters of James Joyce* (London: Faber and Faber, 1975), p. 241.

12. Ellmann's biography includes a table listing the dates of completion for the different episodes. Ellmann, *James Joyce,* p. 456.

13. Ellmann, ed., *Selected Letters,* p. 284.

14. Ibid., pp. 238–39, 251–52, 278, 285.

15. See T. S. Eliot, ed., *Literary Essays of Ezra Pound* (London: Faber and Faber, 1954), p. 9.

16. In "Hades" Bloom wonders about Mr. Power, "Who knows is that true about the woman he keeps?" (77); a few moments later he thinks ruefully of the fact that Martin Cunningham's wife is an "awful drunkard" who pawns the furniture on him (80).

17. Lawrence makes this point explicitly about the method of "Wandering Rocks," but her study implies that the same principle is operative elsewhere in the later episodes. See Karen Lawrence, *The Odyssey of Style in "Ulysses"* (Princeton, N.J.: Princeton University Press, 1981), p. 88.

18. Michael Bell, *The Sentiment of Reality: Truth of Feeling in the European Novel* (London: George Allen & Unwin, 1983), p. 174.

19. Clive Hart and David Hayman, eds., *James Joyce's "Ulysses": Critical Essays* (Berkeley: University of California Press, 1974).

20. Robert Janusko, *The Sources and Structures of James Joyce's "Oxen"* (Ann Arbor, Mich.: UMI Research Press, 1983).

21. See Raleigh, "On the Way Home to Ithaca: The Functions of the 'Eumaeus' Section in *Ulysses*" in Zack Bowen, ed., *Irish Renaissance Annual II* (London and Toronto: Associated University Presses, 1981); pp. 13–114; see also Raleigh, *The Chronicle of Leopold and Molly Bloom: "Ulysses" as Narrative* (Berkeley: University of California Press, 1977).

22. Hugh Kenner suggests something similar when he charts the progress of a mischievous narrator through the book; see Kenner, *Joyce's Voices* (London: Faber and Faber, 1978), pp. 64–99.

23. It was Richard Ellmann, after all, who prophetically anticipated the most celebrated textual restoration in Hans Walter Gabler's 1984 edition of *Ulysses* by announcing that the "word known to all men" (474), which Stephen asks his mother's ghost to tell him, is love. In his recent studies of *Ulysses* Hugh Kenner has used his formidable talents to help us read many obscure signs of Bloom's humanity; for example, he has observed that Bloom is "virtually in shock" over the affair with Boylan and that the most flamboyant styles recount events of the afternoon and evening which, with the exception of the meeting with Stephen, he will suppress when he tells Molly about his day. See Ellmann, *Ulysses on the Liffey*, p. 147; *Ulysses: A Critical and Synoptic Edition*, ed. Hans Walter Gabler et al. (New York: Garland Publishing, 1984), pp. 418–19; Kenner, *Ulysses* (George Allen & Unwin, 1980), pp. 51, 101–2.

Chapter 1

1. Edmund Wilson, *Axel's Castle: A Study in the Imaginative Literature of 1870–1930* (New York: Charles Scribner's Sons, 1931; rpt. London: Collins-Fontana, 1961), pp. 172–73.

2. Lawrence, *The Odyssey of Style in "Ulysses,"* p. 43.

3. *Letters of James Joyce,* Vol. 1, ed. Stuart Gilbert (London: Faber and Faber, 1957), p. 129.

4. Marilyn French makes this comparison one of the premises of her book. French, *The Book as World: James Joyce's "Ulysses,"* pp. 3–22.

5. Marilyn French argues that "Stephen's ironic mode of thought, taken to extremes" determines the narrative tone of the middle sections of *Ulysses* (roughly, from "Sirens" to "Circe") when a "satirical voice" comes to the fore to attack "the ludicrousness of human emotions." See *The Book as World,* pp. 14, 18.

6. Frank O'Connor, *The Lonely Voice: A Study of the Short Story* (Cleveland: The World Publishing Company, 1962), pp. 116–17.

7. Marilyn French also emphasizes the fact that Joyce was not as aesthete. See *The Book as World*, p. 30.

8. Virginia Woolf, *A Writer's Diary* (London: Hogarth Press, 1953), p. 50.

9. *Ulysses: A Critical and Synoptic Edition*, p. 102.

10. Richard Ellmann neatly revised Eliot's statement and applied it to "Oxen of the Sun," arguing that the pastiches show "the utility" of all style. *Ulysses on the Liffey*, p. 135.

11. Ibid., p. 38.

12. The apparition in "Calypso" follows the waste land vision that the Agendath Netaim advertisement in Dlugacz's newspaper prompted. The De Quincey passage in "Oxen of the Sun" features a similar vision (also linked to Agendath Netaim), which is dispelled by the appearance of "Millicent, the young, the dear, the radiant" who is "shod in sandals of bright gold" and is associated with celestial light (338). Also, a stage direction in "Circe" describes Milly as "*fairhaired*" and "*slimsandalled*" (442). I will deal with these images in detail in chapters 5 and 6, respectively.

13. See, for example, pp. 51, 54–55, 74, 304, 568–69.

14. Wilson, *Axel's Castle*, p. 172.

15. *Ulysses: A Critical and Synoptic Edition*, p. 156.

Chapter 2

1. E. M. Forster, *Aspects of the Novel* (London: Edward Arnold, 1927), p. 158.

2. Ellmann and Kenner both imply as much. Ellmann suggests that the headlines could be ascribed to "the omniscient author of traditional fiction, back now in motley instead of his old sober attire," while Kenner remarks that Joyce needed to develop a method that could contain Stephen and Bloom without becoming "Victorian fictionist's puppetry." *Ulysses on the Liffey*, p. 73; Kenner, *Ulysses*, p. 63.

3. On the way to Glasnevin Bloom's composure is tested by the appearance of Boylan (76), the sight of a child's "tiny coffin" (79) and the pious platitudes about suicide he must listen to (79). At the funeral he virtually anatomizes mortality, conjuring up amusing images of resurrection as a scramble for missing body parts (87) and death as an inquiring official at the door (91).

4. R. M. Adams claims that "a great hollow resonance" and "an immense emptiness" permeate Bloom's thoughts in "Hades." Adams, "Hades" in Clive Hart and David Hayman, eds., *James Joyce's "Ulysses": Critical Essays*, pp. 96–97. Still, Bloom's gregariousness and the nimbleness of his mind are as much in evidence here as anywhere else. He introduces the anecdote about Reuben J. Dodd's son (78) and ventures his idea of a tramline "from the parkgate to the quays" (81), something he considered in "Calypso" (47). The busy practicality of his reflections at Glasnevin is comic: he thinks of burying people standing up to save space (89) and equipping coffins with telephones for the benefit of those who might accidentally have been buried alive (91).

5. Writing in 1918 and 1919, respectively, Pound and Woolf had only seen the *Little Review* portions of the book. Pound, "Joyce" in Forrest Read, ed., *Pound/Joyce: The Letters of Ezra Pound to James Joyce with Pound's Essays on Joyce* (London: Faber and Faber, 1968), p. 140; Woolf, "Modern Fiction" in *Collected Essays, Volume Two* (London: Hogarth Press, 1966), p. 107.

6. Many critics have commented on the way the devices of ''Aeolus'' foreshadow the second half of the book. It is certainly as much a self-consciously woven verbal web as, say, ''Oxen of the Sun'' or ''Circe'': this is what prompts Marilyn French to cite it as the first unequivocal notice we are given that *Ulysses* will be an ''epic of relativity.'' Examining the ironic counter-points of the chapter she concludes, ''No one position if unambivalently right, no perspective can contain the whole.'' Among the specific characteristics she points to as evidence are the chiasmus about the ''grassbooted draymen'' (96) and Stephen's parable. Like Karen Lawrence, she sees the former as a stylistic ''preview'' of ''Sirens.'' French claims that the parable ''is written in the voice that dominates the last half of *Ulysses*,'' that of the hangman god or *dio boia*. French, *The Book as World*, pp. 17, 98, 99; Lawrence, *The Odyssey of Style*, p. 69. Hugh Kenner has noted several connections between the verbal play of ''Aeolus'' and that of ''Sirens'' and ''Cyclops.'' For instance, he suggests that the mischievous commentary of the headlines can be related to the tendency of the narrative in ''Sirens'' to refer to passages from earlier in the book. Along with Karen Lawrence, Kenner has also compared the headlines to the inter-ruptions of the second narrator in ''Cyclops.'' Finally, he has observed that, taken out of con-text, some of the Citizen's rhetoric could be mistaken for Professor MacHugh's or vice versa. Kenner, *Joyce's Voices*, pp. 75–76, 77; Kenner, *Ulysses*, p. 100; Lawrence, *The Odyssey of Style*, p. 57.

7. Ellmann emphasizes how normative the roles played by Stephen and Bloom are. See *Ulysses on the Liffey*, pp. 62–73.

8. *The Odyssey of Style*, p. 63.

9. Stephen quotes himself (109, 113), Mr. Deasy (109), Mulligan (110) and Father Dolan from the *Portrait* (111).

10. Simon's gibe was added in its entirety to the first set of proofs. The exchange between Lenehan and O'Madden Burke was altered in two ways: the word ''sphinx'' was substituted for ''vague'' on the third set of proofs and ''reriddled'' replaced ''repeated'' on the sixth set of proofs. See Gabler, et al., *Ulysses: a Critical and Synoptic Edition*, pp. 256, 278. Michael Groden pro-vides an exhaustive account of the evolution of ''Aeolus,'' in *Ulysses in Progress* (Princeton, N.J.: Princeton University Press, 1977), pp. 64–114.

11. Lawrence sees a preview of the stage directions of ''Circe'' in these sentences. *The Odyssey of Style*, p. 150.

12. M. J. C. Hodgart has suggested that Aeolus ''can be read as a one-act play, with very full stage directions and minute instructions to the actors on how to use their bodies.'' Hodgart, ''Aeolus'' in *James Joyce's ''Ulysses'': Critical Essays*, p. 128.

13. Karen Lawrence and Robert Kellogg both conclude that the narrator's antics in this episode emanate from what Kellogg calls ''Stephen's powerfully patterned imagination.'' *The Odyssey of Style*, p. 81; Kellogg, '''Scylla and Charybdis'' in *James Joyce's ''Ulysses'': Critical Essays*, p.159.

14. This levelling effect is quite like the ''chain of mockery'' Lawrence discerns in ''Aeolus'' where the mockers of Dan Dawson are in turn mocked by the headlines. *The Odyssey of Style*, p. 73.

15. Kenner, *Ulysses*, p. 113.

16. Clive Hart outlines a number of good reasons not to trust the interior monologues of ''Wander-ing Rocks.'' Hart, ''Wandering Rocks'' in *James Joyce's ''Ulysses'': Critical Essays*, pp. 190–92.

17. See 1 Kings 18:44–45, 19:12–18.

18. The passage in question concerns Shakespeare walking "greyedauburn" in "Gerard's rosery of Fetter lane" (166, 230). Kenner mentions it in both of his recent studies. *Joyce's Voices,* p. 76; *Ulysses,* p. 64.

19. Describing this quality, Hart contends that the narrator of this episode "reports, but rarely condescends to explain, conceals and reveals according to whim, and both we and the characters suffer from his totalitarian dominance." "Wandering Rocks," *James Joyce's "Ulysses": Critical Essays,* p. 190.

20. See 1 Kings 21:19. There is a stray reference to this episode in "Scylla and Charybdis" when, hearing Mulligan's voice, Stephen repeats to himself the words Ahab utters when Elijah comes to confront him about the murder of Naboth, "Hast thou found me, O mine enemy?" (162). See 1 Kings 21:20. So it is not fanciful to look to the Elijah story for parallels to the relationship of Mulligan and Stephen.

21. This is French's reading. *The Book as World,* p. 121.

22. See 1 Kings 17:8–16.

23. See 1 Kings 19.

24. Lawrence pays an eloquent tribute to this perversity when she says that this episode "investigates the possibilities that are ousted by conventional novelistic plot." *The Odyssey of Style,* p. 88.

25. Ellmann and Stuart Gilbert register this correspondence. *Ulysses on the Liffey,* p. 98; Stuart Gilbert, *James Joyce's "Ulysses": A Study* (New York: Alfred A. Knopf, 1930; rpt. New York: Vintage Books, 1952), p. 239. Ellmann's schema lists Elijah as a "dominant symbol" in the chapter. *Ulysses on the Liffey,* p. 119.

26. Allan Wade, ed., *The Letters of W. B. Yeats* (London: Rupert Hart Davis, 1954), p. 679.

27. This is R. P. Blackmur's phrase for the effect of Stephen's parable. "The Jew in Search of a Son: Joyce's *Ulysses*" in *Eleven Essays in the European Novel* (New York: Harcourt, Brace & World, 1964), p. 42.

Chapter 3

1. See Ellmann, *Ulysses on the Liffey,* p. 151.

2. Marilyn French bases her study of *Ulysses* on the supposition that "uncertainty is . . . built into the entire novel." She argues that the novel is "an epic of relativity" and that the games played with language "undermine every apparent certitude." In the styles of the later episodes Karen Lawrence sees a breaking down of the borders of literature to embrace the "subliterary" in the various forms of newspaper headlines, journalistic parodies, clichés and legalistic or scientific documentation. French, *The Book as World,* p. 17; Lawrence, *The Odyssey of Style,* pp. 79, 110, 178, 180.

3. Stuart Gilbert explains that in the episode's fugal structure Boylan represents "the *Counter-Subject.*" *James Joyce's "Ulysses": A Study,* p. 253.

4. John Paul Riquelme states that "for Bloom, the most important singing occurs not in the Ormond Bar but in his mind, in the memory of his first meeting with Molly." *Teller and Tale in Joyce's Fiction: Oscillating Perspectives* (Baltimore: Johns Hopkins University Press, 1983), p. 211.

5. Ellmann detects hints here of the reservations about the power of music that Bloom will articulate when Ben Dollard sings "The Croppy Boy." *Ulysses on the Liffey,* p. 105.

6. Dan Dawson's speech refers to the *"pensive bosom"* of a *"purling rill"* (102). He also speaks of *"the glowing orb of the moon"* shining forth *"to irradiate her silver effulgence"* (104). In "Lestrygonians" these phrases are conflated by Bloom as "the pensive bosom of the silver effulgence" (132). Then, seeing Lizzie Twigg's loose stockings, he thinks that "literary etherial people" are "dreamy, cloudy, symbolistic" (136).

7. Mark Shechner argues that "Joyce at some point during the composition of *Ulysses* ceased to be bothered by the problem of control and began to emancipate his expansive tendencies without anxieties." According to Shechner, this process entailed a shift from closure to openness and from exclusiveness to inclusiveness in the evolving prose of *Ulysses*. *Joyce in Nighttown: A Psychoanalytic Inquiry into "Ulysses"* (Berkeley: University of California Press, 1974), pp. 135, 137.

8. Karen Lawrence makes the rather imprecise claim that during the interruptions "the forward motion of the linear narrative is halted." Such a claim inadvertently reinforces Edmund Wilson's dismayingly shortsighted judgment that "the gigantic interpolations of the Cyclops episode defeat their object by making it impossible for us to follow the narrative." Lawrence, *The Odyssey of Style,* p. 111; Wilson, *Axel's Castle,* p. 214.

9. Acknowledging that the cinematic splicing began in "Wandering Rocks," Hugh Kenner observes that the frequency of the effect in "Sirens" causes it to resemble "not interpolation but counterpoint." Kenner, *Ulysses,* p. 91.

10. Weldon Thornton perceives an echo of Yeats's play *Cathleen Ni Houlihan* in this sentence. Thornton, *Allusions in "Ulysses": An Annotated List* (Chapel Hill: The University of North Carolina Press, 1968), p. 20.

11. Stuart Gilbert astutely describes the method of "Cyclops" as "the inflation of certain themes to bursting-point, or the projection of Cyclopean shadows of human forms on the sides of a cavern." Both James H. Maddox and Colin MacCabe, in their respective studies, respond to the distortions of this episode by pointing out that the spectacle of two ironic discourses forces the reader to fill in a rational, mediating discourse of his own which will put the events of the chapter in perspective. Gilbert, *James Joyce's "Ulysses",* p. 274; Maddox, *Joyce's "Ulysses" and the Assault upon Character* (New Brunswick, N.J.: Rutgers University Press, 1978), p. 88; MacCabe, *James Joyce and the Revolution of the Word* (London: MacMillan, 1978), pp. 90–93.

12. Herbert Schneidau has noted that in "Cyclops" "the dialogue is separate from the reporting of it." Schneidau, "One Eye and Two Levels: On Joyce's 'Cyclops,'" *James Joyce Quarterly* Vol. 16, nos. 1/2 (Fall 1978/Winter 1979), 99.

13. Of course, as I suggested in chapter 2, Bloom's interior monologue offsets the dialogue of more public episodes like "Hades" and "Aeolus" in the same way that the parodic stage directions offset the naturalistic exchanges in "Cyclops."

14. Of the thirty-two interruptions in the episode, seven can be read as pieces of narration. The final one, which is the longest and also the only one not mentioned in this discussion, is the stretch of dialogue dramatizing the arrival of Martin Cunningham, Jack Power and Crofton at the pub (275–76).

15. With regard to the relationship between playfulness and the formal elaborations of *Ulysses* Anthony Cronin has written: "The imagination will not function without a framework of some sort. . . . Nor indeed should it be forgotten that in every use of form as well as in every extension of allusion there is an element of play, that element of play which paradoxically deepens the being of a work of art and without which the composition of works of art on the scale of

Ulysses would scarcely be possible." In her brilliant study of the role of parody in modern art forms Linda Hutcheon traces the sort of flexibility we have celebrated in the Cyclopean interruptions to a duality in the word's etymology: the Greek prefix *para* can mean not only "counter" or "against" but "beside" as well. Hutcheon sees in the latter connotation "a suggestion of an accord or intimacy instead of a contrast" and claims that the irony which thus results "can be playful as well as belittling." Cronin, *A Question of Modernity* (London: Secker and Warburg, 1966), p. 66; Hutcheon, *A Theory of Parody: The Teachings of Twentieth-Century Art Forms*, p. 32.

Chapter 4

1. In her sympathetic reading of "Nausicaa" Suzette Henke sees Gerty as a victim of her environment. Henke praises Gerty for her powers of creative compensation: "She imaginatively interprets her existence in the mode of sentimental romance, using it to mitigate a reality that otherwise might prove intolerable. . . . Her fantasies may be pathetic and futile, but they appear to be crucial to her mental well-being. . . . Like Leopold Bloom, Gerty sustains herself through the copious creations of a fertile imagination." "Gerty MacDowell: Joyce's Sentimental Heroine" in Suzette Henke and Elaine Unkeless, eds., *Women in Joyce* (Urbana: University of Illinois Press, 1982), pp. 133–37.

2. Fritz Senn maintains that the style of Gerty's section is not "as monotonous or uniform as critics have assumed." He writes: "The tone keeps changing within a limited range so that the chapter is one of those characterized by the marvellously attuned wrong note." Senn, "Nausicaa" in Hart and Hayman, eds., *James Joyce's "Ulysses": Critical Essays*, pp. 305–6.

3. Bonnie Kime Scott says that the conditions of Gerty's life are "grim" and that Bloom represents the "nurturing male" who appears in the kind of romance literature she reads. Scott, *James Joyce* (Brighton: Harvester Press, 1987), p. 64.

4. Stuart Gilbert astutely links the scathing irony created by the linoleum slogans to the Homeric parallel, pointing out that the "standard designs, fit for a palace" are a faint reproduction of "the wonders of the palace of Alcinous" in *The Odyssey*. Gilbert, *James Joyce's "Ulysses": A Study*, p. 289.

5. It is interesting that the one poem Gerty refers to is quoted in *Stephen Hero* and features a madonna with an infant, so the church is a source of imagery as well as spiritual consolation. With regard to Gerty's taste for poetry Richard Ellmann correctly states: "Joyce was Tolstoyan, he respected simplicity, he thought simple people were not divorced from artistic capacity." See Joyce, *Stephen Hero*, ed. John J. Slocum and Herbert Cahoon (New York: New Directions, 1944, 1963), p. 83; Ellmann, *Ulysses on the Liffey*, p. 130.

6. Despite her feminist convictions, Marilyn French judges Gerty rather harshly and is willing to identify her completely with the discourse in which she is presented: "Gerty's sentimental and romantic notions are an ironic comment on the bleak life she lives, and her actual inadequacy, her moral and physical lameness." Suzette Henke's portrayal of Gerty as a prisoner of a "manipulative society" and a "media-controlled self-image" is far more sympathetic. French, *The Book as World*, p. 168; Henke, pp. 134–35.

7. When Gerty takes off her hat the narrator says: "and a prettier, a daintier head of nutbrown tresses was never seen on a girl's shoulders" (295).

8. Gilbert lists the technique of "Nausicaa" as "Tumescence: detumescence." *James Joyce's "Ulysses": A Study*, p. 278.

9. In his chapter on the Uncle Charles Principle, Hugh Kenner devotes several insightful pages to what he calls Gerty's "expressive disarray." See *Joyce's Voices,* pp. 17–20.

10. Kenner points out that Gerty's exhibition of her underwear and the exhibition of the sacrament are "synchronized." Hugh Kenner, *Dublin's Joyce* (London: Chatto and Windus, 1955), p. 258.

11. One series of fragmented sentences in "Sirens" includes references to Boylan riding along the quays, Bloom and Richie Goulding eating, Simon Dedalus and Father Cowley conversing and the barmaids pining (221).

12. In a provocative article Patrick McGee treats Joyce's submersion in a female consciousness in "Nausicaa" as a spirited act of writing. McGee says: "To state it (not quite) metaphorically, the free indirect style of 'Nausicaa' is Joyce's nausea: his incorporation into the body of literature of the writing that literature excludes, that falls below the standard of the *mot juste.* I would argue that to read the Gerty section of 'Nausicaa' as Joyce's rather awkward attempt to represent a young woman (whether we take Gerty to be just past seventeen or almost twenty-two) is to miss the point. Joyce knows, more or less, how to characterize young women as we see, for instance, in 'Eveline.' In 'Nausucaa,' however, he is doing something else; he is reproducing the literary man's nausea; he is rewriting the style of another that both seduces and repulses him, and he is reinvesting that style with his own desire even as he allows his own desire to be reinformed by the style. In effect, he 'represents' a representation and discloses not only the imaginary view of the world supporting the representation but the order of literary conventions permitting him to portray that view as imaginary." McGee's claim that the ironic light in "Nausicaa" reflects upon all the levels of its literary creation refutes Karen Lawrence's allegation that the first part of the episode vitiates "the pluralism of the text" by suggesting "that there is some Olympian ground upon which the writer and the reader can stand to be exempt from the charges of stupidity." Patrick McGee, "Joyce's Nausea: Style and Representation in 'Nausicaa,'" *James Joyce Quarterly* Vol. 24, no. 3 (Spring 1987), 308–9; Lawrence, *The Odyssey of Style in "Ulysses,"* pp. 122–23.

13. See Ellmann, *Ulysses on the Liffey,* pp. 126–27; Henke, p. 136; Lawrence, *The Odyssey of Style in "Ulysses,"* p. 119; McGee, p. 307; Senn, p. 296.

14. Sonia Orwell and Ian Angus, eds., *The Collected Essays, Journalism and Letters of George Orwell, Volume I: An Age Like This, 1920–1940* (London: Secker and Warburg, 1968), p. 128.

15. Suzette Henke writes: "Gerty's 'little strangled cry' may be an unwitting moan of sexual frustration. Gerty seems to linger in tumescent ecstasy, passionately aroused and tortured by the sweet pain of unconsummated desire." Henke, p. 145.

16. Interestingly, Joyce added the four phrases that elaborate Gerty's cry with such obvious relish to the typescript and proofs of the episode. See *Ulysses: A Critical and Synoptic Edition,* p. 788.

17. James H. Maddox observes that neither character comes off particularly well in "Nausicaa." He writes: "This is one of those instances when Joyce's parody is almost totally destructive in its double-edged power. It reminds us at once of the fatuity of adolescence and the futility of maturity." Maddox, *Joyce's "Ulysses" and the Assault upon Character,* p. 79.

18. Fritz Senn relates Gerty's style to the "language of flowers" (64) Bloom improvises after reading Martha's letter. Senn, p. 298.

Chapter 5

1. W. B. Yeats, *Essays and Introductions* (London: MacMillan, 1961), p. 28.

2. Interestingly, in the letter to Harriet Shaw Weaver defending the technique of "Sirens," Joyce wrote that "in the compass of one day to compress all these wanderings and *clothe* them in the form of this day is for me only possible by such variation which, I beg you to believe, is not capricious" (my italics). *Letters of James Joyce,* ed. Stuart Gilbert. p. 129.

3. First of all, the words "last lonely" in the first sentence of the paragraph quoted were mistakenly changed to "long lost" by Joyce and his typist, a misreading that survived until Gabler's 1984 edition. Also, the phrase "hour of folding" has been misprinted as "hour of holding" since 1926. See Gabler's *Ulysses: A Critical and Synoptic Edition,* pp. 814, 1744, 1798. For manuscripts and typescripts see the volume entitled *Ulysses: "Wandering Rocks," "Sirens," "Cyclops," and "Nausicaa." A Facsimile of Manuscripts and Typescripts for Episodes 10–13,* in *The James Joyce Archive,* ed. Michael Groden (New York: Garland Publishing, 1977). For proofs see the volume entitled *Ulysses: "Sirens," "Cyclops," "Nausicaa," and "Oxen of the Sun." A Facsimile of Placards for Episodes 11–14,* in *The James Joyce Archive,* ed. Michael Groden (New York: Garland Publishing, 1978).

4. Because the formal effects of "Nausicaa" are less spectacular than those of "Cyclops" and "Oxen of the Sun," critics have been less inclined to examine the nuances in the tone of the narrative as it wavers between Gerty and Bloom. Marilyn French acknowledges the existence of a narrator who "stands above" both Gerty and Bloom and notes that parts of Bloom's section "take place outside his consciousness, although they are here, as in Sirens, woven into his monologue." Like French, Fritz Senn detects a sense of compassionate moral ambivalence in the chapter's juxtaposition of viewpoints. French and Senn both note in passing the shift in tone of the paragraph I have examined. French, *The Book as World,* pp. 166–67; Senn, "Nausicaa" in *James Joyce's "Ulysses": Critical Essays,* ed. Clive Hart and David Hayman, pp. 278–81, 304, 310–11.

5. Lawrence recognizes the fact that in "Oxen" there is a degree of self-consciousness in the narrative that greatly exceeds that of the omniscient narrator in any conventional novel. She writes: "As in 'Aeolus,' Joyce plays with language as quotation, a field of repetition that includes: the characters unwittingly, wittingly, and sometimes, wittily quoting themselves, each other, and literature, and the book quoting lines from its own previous pages and from other writers. Increasingly, the characters' memories and the narrative memory fuse—at a certain level, all the 'memories' in the book are fictions created out of other fictions for the purpose of this fiction. All are quotations or citations, iterative events, linguistic and dramatic, including the title of the book that prepares us to encounter a retelling of a very old story." *The Odyssey of Style in Ulysses,* p. 141.

6. Wolfgang Iser remarks that "Oxen of the Sun" dramatizes "the inadequacy of style as regards the presentation of reality." Marilyn French echoes this judgment with her conclusion that it is a chapter about literature in which "literary expression is shown to be inadequate to confer certitude, incapable of rendering ultimate reality." Hugh Kenner defines style as "a system of limits" and points out that pastiche and parody "test the limits of someone else's system of perception." Finally, in a refreshingly irreverent essay, Leslie Fiedler says that "Oxen" is "Joyce's climactic onslaught against literature" and asks, "What else except hostility to the whole of 'Eng. Lit.' could have motivated that deliberately boring series of pastiche-travesties . . . unless its point be the pointlessness of *all* style, of the very notion of style, and certainly the study of it." Iser, *The Implied Reader: Patterns of Communication in Prose Fiction from Bunyan to Beckett* (Baltimore: Johns Hopkins University Press, 1974), p. 192; French, *The Book as World,* p. 169; Kenner, *Joyce's Voices,* p. 81; Fiedler, "To Whom Does Joyce Belong? *Ulysses* as Parody, Pop and Porn" in Heyward Ehrlich, ed., *Light Rays: James Joyce and Modernism* (New York: New Horizon Press, 1984), p. 36.

7. There are two echoes of the Malory passage in "Penelope." On both occasions Molly thinks of the jacket she knitted for Rudy (610, 640). The Pater paragraph recalls the evening at Mat Dillon's when Bloom annoyed John Henry Menton, an incident witnessed by Molly as well as Stephen and his mother. Menton and Bloom remember the scene in "Hades" (88, 94–95); later, in "Ithaca" and "Penelope" respectively, Bloom and Molly reflect upon the fact that Stephen was there (556, 637). John Henry Raleigh pronounces it "the most extensive multiple memory in the book." See *The Chronicle of Leopold and Molly Bloom: "Ulysses" as Narrative*, p. 80.

8. Recent critics have relied heavily on J. S. Atherton's indispensible study of "Oxen of the Sun" in which plenty of evidence is furnished to support the suggestion that Joyce "deliberately confused his margins so as to make it impossible to produce an accurate tabulation of the various details in his chapter." Marilyn French ingeniously relates the chapter to her conviction that Joyce "shows sexuality, like every other human concern, to be rooted in the void, in a great unknowingness"; specifically she argues that "just as prophylaxis sterilizes coition, any style to some extent sterilizes the coition of the act and the word." She concludes: "No course of action in sexual life can lead to salvation, just as none of the many styles leads to certitude about reality." It has even been demonstrated that Joyce's parodies clash with their supposed originals. Kenner portrays Joyce as "working against the grain of his parodies" and illustrates his point by deftly analyzing a paragraph in the style of Macaulay. Similarly, Karen Lawrence shows how the imitation of Newman subtly deviates from its model. J. S. Atherton, "The Oxen of the Sun" in *James Joyce's "Ulysses": Critical Essays,* ed. Clive Hart and David Hayman, p. 323; French, *The Book as World,* pp. 50, 172, 182; Kenner, *Joyce's Voices,* pp. 48–49, 106–9; Lawrence, *The Odyssey of Style in "Ulysses,"* pp. 141–43.

9. Stuart Gilbert notes that Stephen's speech resembles the "Reproaches" from the Good Friday mass. *James Joyce's "Ulysses": A Study,* pp. 300–2.

10. Although Atherton mentions Milton as a possible model for a couple of passages in the vicinity of Stephen's Biblical apostrophe, the apostrophe itself does not resemble any of the Milton selections in either Saintsbury or Peacock, the two principal sources Atherton cites for Joyce's imitations. However, in the Rosenbach manuscript of *Ulysses* this passage contains the phrase "bitter ashes" which recalls the incident in *Paradise Lost* (X, 566) in which the Satanic host, having been momentarily transformed into serpents after the fall and confronted with a forbidden tree, find that the fruit tastes of "bitter ashes." Atherton, op. cit. George Saintsbury, *A History of English Prose Rhythm* (London: MacMillan, 1912), pp. 168–76. W. Peacock, *English Prose from Mandeville to Ruskin* (London: Grant Richards, 1903), pp. 86–87. For the Rosenbach manuscript see *Ulysses: A Facsimile of the Manuscript,* ed. Clive Driver (London: Faber and Faber, 1975).

11. *Hamlet,* 3. 4. 93–95.

12. Declan Kiberd relates Stephen and Bloom's Eastern dreams to the line from Yeats about the shifting borders of our minds. *Men and Feminism in Modern Literature* (London: MacMillan, 1985), pp. 177, 184, 188.

13. See *Ulysses: A Critical and Synoptic Edition,* pp. 360, 1270.

14. Kenner, *Ulysses,* p. 115. Kenner also compares *Ulysses* to a detective story and provides a good commentary on the motifs in the Gothic passage. Ibid., pp. 80–81, 121–23.

15. For the genesis of the Gothic passage see Gabler et al., pp. 886–88 and the volume entitled *Ulysses: "Oxen of the Sun" and "Circe." A Facsimile of Drafts, Manuscripts and Typescripts for Episodes 14 and 15* in *The James Joyce Archive,* ed. Michael Groden.

16. Ellmann and Kenner both detect suggestions of such a microcosm in "Calypso." See Ellmann, *Ulysses on the Liffey,* p. 38 and Kenner, *Ulysses,* p. 47.

17. Weldon Thornton cites the Litany as one of the main sources for the Mariolatry of "Nausicaa" and discerns echoes of it in the De Quincey pastiche. *Allusions in Ulysses,* pp. 306, 309, 311, 312, 319, 343. Also, Eugene Webb cites the vision of Milly as an example of the rebirth of "the starlike flower of the transfiguring ideal" in a "desert of profane secularity." *The Dark Dove: The Sacred and Secular in Modern Literature* (Seattle: University of Washington Press, 1975), p. 135.

18. T. S. Eliot, ed., *Literary Essays of Ezra Pound,* p. 9.

19. T. S. Eliot praised Joyce for using allusions to open vistas to the imagination. See the review in *Today* (September 1918) which is quoted by David Perkins in *A History of Modern Poetry* (Cambridge, Mass.: Belknap Press of Harvard University Press, 1976), p. 477.

Chapter 6

1. Patrick A. McCarthy describes "Circe" as "narration masquerading as drama." "Non-Dramatic Illusion in 'Circe' " in J. Aubert and M. Jolas, eds., *Joyce and Paris 1902 . . . 1920–1940 . . . 1975: Papers from the Fifth International James Joyce Symposium* (Paris: Publications de l'Université de Lille, 1979), p. 25.

2. Richard Ellmann, ed., *Selected Letters of James Joyce,* p. 83.

3. Noting Stephen's assertion, Zack Bowen writes: "The emphasis has shifted from the *word* in 'Oxen' to the *gesture* in 'Circe.' " "Ulysses" in Zack Bowen and James F. Carens, eds., *A Companion to Joyce Studies* (Westport, Conn.: Greenwood Press, 1984), p. 519.

4. With regard to the narrative technique of "Circe," John Paul Riquelme remarks: "In 'Circe' we hve only the ghost of the initial style. Joyce presses the issue of the narrator's impersonality by evoking contradictory implications. He emphasizes the possibility of a transparent, or objective, presentation independent of the author by casting the episode in the trappings of drama, with typography suggesting direct discourse. But the details of style, especially the changes in register, suggest instead the narrator's presence by stressing the act of narrating." *Teller and Tale in Joyce's Fiction,* p. 140.

5. Marilyn French notes that the stage directions occasionally contain reversions to the narrative voices of "Sirens," "Cyclops" and "Nausicaa." Patrick A. McCarthy likens the hallucinations to the interruptions in "Cyclops." French, *The Book as World,* p. 195; McCarthy, op. cit.

6. In an important article Mackie L. Jarrell explores Joyce's use of proverbs from Swift's *Polite Conversation* in "Circe" and concludes that Zoe Higgins speaks more of them than any other character. Jarrell, "Joyce's Use of Swift's *Polite Conversation* in the 'Circe' Episode of *Ulysses,*" *PMLA* 72 (1957), 545–54.

7. Hugh Kenner has remarked upon the fact that this direction becomes progressively more lyrical. Kenner, *Ulysses,* p. 123.

8. In a letter to Frank Budgen Joyce described the moly Hermes gives to Odysseus as "the invisible influence (prayer, chance, agility, presence of mind, power of recuperation) which saves in case of accident." In the case of Bloom, Joyce continued, the "plant may be said to have many leaves, indifference due to masturbation, pessimism congenital, a sense of the ridiculous, sudden fastidiousness in some detail, experience." Anthony Cronin speaks of Bloom's "continuing courage" and points out that in him we "recognize that here is the familiar: the worn,

familiar, comical, shabby, eroded but not collapsed face of humanity.'' Cronin also writes movingly of Bloom's ''continous but uncertain ability to remain upright.'' Ellmann, ed., *Selected Letters*, p. 272; Cronin, *A Question of Modernity*, pp. 93–94.

9. Frank Budgen wisely declares that the ''daydream is the native element of the poor man'' while Mark Shechner claims that ''Joyce's own theories about the moral equivalent of Bloom's moly are not really incommensurable with the idea that moly may be fantasy itself'' and that ''Bloom's fantasy life is therapeutic.'' Frank Budgen, *James Joyce and the Making of ''Ulysses''* (London: Grayson and Grayson, 1934), p. 244. Mark Shechner, *Joyce in Nighttown: A Psychoanalytic Inquiry into ''Ulysses,''* pp. 117, 123.

10. Adaline Glasheen offers an excellent commentary on Bloom's encounter with the nymph. ''Calypso'' in Hart and Jayman, eds., *James Joyce's ''Ulysses'': Critical Essays*, pp. 61–70.

11. It hardly seems sufficient merely to say, as Bowen does, that these are ''stock pictures of innocence and goodness.'' Bowen, p. 521.

12. William Peden has contended that the spirit of ''Circe'' is fundamentally affirmative, that it is ''Chaucerian, not Dantean or Homeric,'' and that it is ''illuminated with a remarkable sense of *gentleness.*'' ''A Note or Two on Form and Content in 'Circe' '' in *Joyce and Paris,* p. 15.

13. It is possible to read this speech as another result of the relationship between Bloom's voice and that of the book's mocking narrator, since Marilyn French identifies Virag as ''a mass of malice, disgust, unusual words and odd facts'' and as ''the incarnation of the narrator of *Ulysses.*'' French, *The Book as World*, p. 204.

14. The initial style's third-person narrator is not given to such easy allusiveness: in fact the only precedent for this is the reference to Darwin in the Burke imitation in ''Oxen'' (333), a strangely familiar touch which, occurring where it does, just adds to the first reader's bewilderment.

15. Ezra Pound and Karen Lawrence have both made helpful remarks about the casual swiftness of the mythologizing in ''Circe.'' Pound rejoiced that ''Circe'' brought harpies, furies and symbols to life without resorting to mythology or dogmatic faith. In a memorable passage Lawrence writes: ''The paradox of 'Circe' is that we do not move beneath convention to the 'real' original selves of the characters or through rhetoric to 'sincerity.' What we realize in the mode of 'Circe' is that the unconscious *is* conventional and rhetorical: in the unconscious, myth and melodrama, archetype and stereotype merge. We play the roles basic to all four: parents, children, lovers, daemons. Somewhere in the dark recesses of his psyche, Stephen is a rebel and redeemer, Bloom a betrayed martyr. 'Circe' helps us to see that the symbolic parallels between the characters and past literary figures are part of the role playing in the uncnscious itself.'' See Pound, ''James Joyce et Pecuchet'' in Forrest Read, ed., *Pound/Joyce*, p. 207. Lawrence, *The Odyssey of Style in ''Ulysses,''* pp. 158–59.

16. Neither Thornton nor Gifford and Seidman list a source for these words. See Thornton, *Allusions in ''Ulysses,''* p. 428. See also, Don Gifford and Robert J. Seidman, *Notes for Joyce: An Annotation of James Joyce's ''Ulysses''* (New York: E. P. Dutton, 1974), p. 433.

17. Ellmann invokes Dante in his reading of this passage, calling Yeats ''Virgil,'' Miss Ferguson ''Beatrice'' and Rudy ''Matilda.'' *Ulysses on the Liffey,* pp. 147–49. See also Dante's *Purgatorio,* Canto 31, lines 88–105.

18. Of course Rudy's *''Eton suit''* and *''mauve face''* (497) can be traced to Bloom's thoughts in ''Hades'' (73, 79).

19. Kenner speaks of Stephen's ''transfiguration'' in this scene. Hugh Kenner, *Dublin's Joyce,* p. 120.

20. For the image of the fading coal see "A Defence of Poetry" in Harry Buxton Forman, ed., *The Prose Works of Percy Bysshe Shelley*, Vol. 3 (London: Reeves and Turner, 1880), p. 137. See also Yeats's definition of a symbol as "a transparent lamp about a spiritual flame" in his *Essays and Introductions*, p. 116.

21. Richard Ellmann, ed., *Selected Letters of James Joyce*, p. 269.

22. Shechner has commented on the fact that most of the action in the episode proceeds from Bloom's mind. He writes: "Bloom carries this inquisitorial apparatus around in his head. He is self-tormented, self-accused, and self-confessed. His penance is self-imposed and his despair self-contained. Bloom has gone forth and it is to Bloom that his steps have tended." Riquelme has correctly asserted that the stage directions and dialogue take on a peculiar textual life of their own, declaring that the "primary fantasy of the episode is the episode itself" and that its "organizing principles, rather than referential ones, are self-referential." These qualities are part and parcel of the form of the episode which, Joyce told Budgen, was governed by "the rhythm of locomotor ataxy." Thus Stuart Gilbert lists "Locomotor Apparatus" as the chapter's organ. Shechner, *Joyce in Nighttown*, p. 116. Riquelme, *Teller and Tale in Joyce's Fiction*, p. 142. Budgen, *James Joyce and the Making of "Ulysses,"* p. 234. Gilbert, *James Joyce's "Ulysses": A Study*, p. 313.

Chapter 7

1. Critics like Hugh Kenner have paid tribute in passing to the liveliness of the episode's style, but it was not until fairly recently, with the publication of John Henry Raleigh's lengthy and provocative study, that "Eumaeus" was given the extended treatment it deserves. Raleigh achieves the twofold purpose of bringing the historical nuances of the chapter into sharp focus and of cataloguing the wide variety of pleasures afforded by its unassuming style. Kenner, *Joyce's Voices*, p. 98; *Ulysses*, p. 130. John Henry Raleigh, "On the Way Home to Ithaca: The Functions of the 'Eumaeus' Section in *Ulysses*" in Zack Bowen, ed., *Irish Renaissance Annual II*, pp. 13–114.

2. Gerald L. Bruns claims that in this episode "the spirit of romance is displaced by the spirit of ordinary life." Bruns, "Eumaeus" in Hart and Hayman, eds., *James Joyce's "Ulysses": Critical Essays*, pp. 363–64.

3. Noting similar suggestions of the narrator's omniscience, Bruns writes of "a kind of fluid presence" and points to the hilariously bungled sketch of Corley's genealogy (504) as an instance in which "it is the narrator himself who is dramatized." There is a hint of such a dramatization in the detail of Murphy's preference for "good old Hollands and water." Bruns, p. 368.

4. Raleigh observes that "Eumaeus" is "a bridge between the world of fantasy and the world of reality, and partakes of the characteristics of each." Raleigh, p. 35.

5. See *Finnegans Wake* (London: Faber and Faber, 1939), pp. 543–45.

6. Raleigh remarks upon the charm of the returned husband's monologue. Raleigh, p. 17.

7. At this point we may be reminded of certain mannerisms in the imitations in "Oxen," like, perhaps, the sentence in the Dickensian treatment of Mrs. Purefoy that exhorts us to "Reverently look at her as she reclines there . . . breathing a silent prayer of thanksgiving to One above, the Universal Husband" (343). There are also shards of Cyclopean and Circean images in the picture of Murphy's return. The identification of the usurper as "Chubb or Tomkin" and the fact that he eats "rumpsteak and onions" provide subliminally precise links with the execution scene

in "Cyclops" where the victim is given "fried steak and onions" for breakfast (254) and where the military supervisor is one "Tomkin-Maxwell" who speaks of returning to his wife, the "old mashtub . . . down Limehouse way" (255). Of course there is Stephen's reference to a musical figure called "Tomkins" (540) at the end of the episode, too. In "Circe," as Bloom's humiliation at the hands of Bello reaches its nadir, he is transformed into Rip Van Winkle looking in the window at a figure he takes to be Molly the first time he saw her at Mat Dillon's in Terenure but which in fact turns out to be Milly (442). Joyce added the better part of the rhetorical imperative and the names "Chubb or Tomkin" to the third and fourth sets of proofs, respectively. The reminiscence of "Oxen" in the former may not be deliberate, but the verbal echo of "Cyclops" in the latter seems too close to be haphazard. See Gabler, ed., *Ulysses: A Critical and Synoptic Edition*, p. 1364.

8. In an interesting essay on "Eumaeus" Alistair Stead points not to treachery but to error as the governing formal and thematic concept in the episode. Stead astutely notes that the "ludicrous carelessness of association" in "Eumaeus" is the "verbal counterpart to the theme of false friendship." He also remarks in passing on the fact that Joyce relates the theme of treachery to linguistic betrayal of reality. Stead, "Reflections on Eumaeus: Ways of Error and Glory in 'Ulysses' " in W. J. McCormack and Alistair Stead, eds., *James Joyce and Modern Literature* (London: Routledge and Kegan Paul, 1982), pp. 143, 156.

9. In "James Joyce et Pecuchet," Ezra Pound speaks of Bloom as "l'homme qui croit ce qu'il lit dans les journaux." Forrest Read, ed., *Pound/Joyce*, p. 206.

10. It is worth noting that the spoken version of the encounter with Parnell gathers together many of the clichés that are sprinkled in the speculative sentences surrounding the unspoken version. Words and phrases like "a commanding figure," "the idol with feet of clay," "trusty henchmen," "mudslinging" and "shillyshally" all appear in the vicinity of the first account and are recycled in the second. So the ostensibly erratic narrative does represent Bloom's thought and speech with some consistency.

11. Karen Lawrence and John Henry Raleigh have both made illuminating observations about the sense of stylistic letting go in "Eumaeus." Lawrence contends that the striving for stylelessness abolishes the whole notion of "condescending irony," since (she writes) "no one, no writer or reader, can remain outside the ring of stupidity Joyce draws." Raleigh notes that the narrative of "Eumaeus" is like that of "Oxen of the Sun" in that it constitutes a burial of subject matter beneath the surface of the page and a disassociation of the author from the telling of his story. Lawrence, *The Odyssey of Style in "Ulysses,"* p. 174. Raleigh, p. 25.

Chapter 8

1. Critics have described the effect of the catechism's encyclopedic style in a variety of ways. In an influential article R. A. Copland and G. W. Turner suggest that the esoteric vocabulary and the question-and-answer format constitute a parodic mask that allows the author to disappear from view. John Henry Raleigh writes of Joyce's disassociation of himself from his subject matter and points out that, although the novel's action is buried "under the surface of the page" in "Oxen of the Sun" and "Eumaeus," this is only partially true of "Ithaca." With regard to the unfolding of the human drama on Eccles Street, S. L. Goldberg claims that the objective of the catechism is "not to demolish Bloom and Stephen into scattered, fragmentary 'facts,' but rather to show their ultimate invulnerability to this view of them." Marilyn French points to the role played by our response, asserting that "the very impersonality of the style . . . confers poignancy on the scene: it draws its emotional content from the reader."

A. Walton Litz and James H. Maddox evoke the rather fugitive relationship in this episode between character and action on the one hand and the poetic resonances of the language on the other. Litz, in a stimulating discussion of the ways in which "Ithaca" subverts and transcends the conventions of realistic fiction, contends that the episode "progresses by a rhythmic alteration between mythic or 'epiphanic' moments and longer stretches of 'realism' which validate these moments." Maddox sees "Ithaca" as a supreme example of Joyce's ability to simultaneously communicate "the immediacy of the action" and draw our attention to "the shape of the language which conveys that action"; he declares that, as such, it "dramatizes the triumph and limitations of the form-making imagination." Karen Lawrence's interpretation also pays tribute to the hard-won consolations of the Ithacan prose: she says that here "lyrical passages . . . are left to stand without becoming parodic" and finds that in the end "a sense of possibility mitigates the alienation of the cosmic perspective." Copland and Turner, "The Nature of James Joyce's Parody in 'Ithaca,' " *Modern Language Review* 64, no. 4 (October 1969), 759–63. Raleigh, "On the Way Home to Ithaca: The Functions of the 'Eumaeus' Section in *Ulysses*" in Zack Bowen, ed., *Irish Renaissance Annual II*, p. 25. Goldberg, *The Classical Temper: A Study of James Joyce's "Ulysses"* (London: Chatto and Windus, 1961), pp. 189–90. French, *The Book as World*, p. 20. Litz, "Ithaca" in Hart and Hayman, eds., *James Joyce's "Ulysses": Critical Essays*, p. 402. Maddox, *Joyce's "Ulysses" and the Assault upon Character*, pp. 186, 188. Lawrence, *The Odyssey of Style*, pp. 185, 201.

2. In a recent article Harold D. Baker alleges that "Stephen's poetic diction can be recognized" in this famous line. "Rite of Passage: 'Ithaca,' Style, and the Structure of *Ulysses*," *James Joyce Quarterly* 23, no. 3 (Spring 1986), 277–97.

3. John Paul Riquelme cmpares the qualified realism of "Eumaeus" and "Ithaca" to that of "Aeolus," which he describes as "a halfway stage that mediates between the initial style and the more extreme various styles." Riquelme goes on to say that the homecoming episodes contain "a selective, but thorough, mixture of earlier stylistic tendencies." *Teller and Tale in Joyce's Fiction*, p. 217.

4. Both Marilyn French and Zack Bowen observe that the method of the catechism incorporates scientific and religious elements and so reflects Bloom and Stephen's different ways of viewing the world. French, *The Book as World*, p. 219. Bowen, "Ulysses" in Zack Bowen and James F. Carens, eds., *A Companion to Joyce Studies*, pp. 539–40.

5. In fact the list of astral colors recalls the "emerald, sapphire, mauve and heliotrope" veil surrounding Milly in the De Quincey pastiche (338). More specifically, cinnabar is actually mentioned in other such lists: Russell the lapidary's shop in "Wandering Rocks" contains "lozenges of cinnabar" and "winedark stones" (198) while the floor of Bella Cohen's musicroom *"is covered with an oilcloth mosaic of jade and azure and cinnabar rhomboids"* (409). So the specialized language of "Ithaca" is not quite as aberrant as it may sometimes seem.

6. Mark E. Littmann and Charles A. Schweighauser link the astronomical language of both the De Quincey pastiche and the scene in Bloom's garden to the theme of paternity in the novel. James H. Maddox reads the astronomy passages as manifestations of the catechism's tendency to "stress the insignificance of the individual unit when it is considered among the infinite set of which it is an integer" and concludes that this tendency is as characteristic of Bloom's interior monologue as it is of "Ithaca." Marilyn French acknowledges the mutability of the cosmos which is pictured in the consideration of the stars, but nevertheless emphasizes the survival of Bloom the "competent keyless citizen" (572) and "conscious reactor against the void of incertitude" (604). Littmann and Schweighauser, "Astronomical Allusions: Their Meaning and Purpose in *Ulysses*," *James Joyce Quarterly* 2, no. 4 (Summer 1965), 238–46. Maddox, *Joyce's "Ulysses" and the Assault upon Character*, pp. 198–99. French, *The Book as World*, pp. 241–42.

7. Stuart Gilbert claims that "the ironic influence of Stephen . . . is discernible" in the consideration of "the posited influence of celestial on human bodies." *James Joyce's "Ulysses": A Study*, p. 377.

8. The Polish novelist Jan Parandowski reports that, in defence of his claim that *Ulysses* was an epic of the human body, Joyce complained that "for too long were the stars studied and man's insides neglected. An eclipse of the sun could be predicted many centuries before anyone knew which way the blood circulated in our bodies." This is probably why Bloom's first thoughts of the stars in "Ithaca" are followed by a reference to "the universe of human serum constellated with red and white bodies" (573). See Parandowski, "Meeting with Joyce" in Willard Potts, ed., *James Joyce: Portraits of the Artist in Exile* (Dublin: Wolfhound Press, 1979), pp. 154–62.

9. In the Linati Schema, the phrase "Pacified Style" is listed as part of the technic of "Ithaca." See Ellmann, *Ulysses on the Liffey*, Appendix. In a letter to Budgen, Joyce said that in "Ithaca" Bloom and Stephen "become heavenly bodies, wanderers like the stars at which they gaze." Ellmann, ed., *Selected Letters of James Joyce*, p. 278.

10. Lawrence notes the use of hypothesis and conjecture in 'Ithaca." *The Odyssey of Style*, p. 192.

11. Harold D. Baker traces some of the poetic liberties Joyce takes with his scientific catechism. Baker's article examines "the various ways in which the facade of objective description in 'Ithaca' is distorted by formal and stylistic devices."

12. Even though this fragmented quotation would seem to contain the very roots of the passage, a glance at Hans Walter Gabler's synoptic edition will reveal that perhaps half of the words I have quoted were added in typescripts or proofs. See Gabler, *Ulysses: A Critical and Synoptic Edition*, p. 1570. Richard Madtes has written a fascinating study of the episode's textual evolution. Madtes, "Joyce and the Building of 'Ithaca,'" *Journal of English Literary History* 31 (1964), 443–59.

13. Maddox calls the creation of Flowerville "a jocoserious triumph of the empirical mind beset by the knowledge of its own futility." *Joyce's "Ulysses" and the Assault upon Character*, p. 199.

14. S. L. Goldberg argues that Ithaca "parodies the method and outlook of naturalistic Realism in order to suggest what lies beyond its grasp." *The Classical Temper*, p. 190.

15. Litz stresses the importance of the fact that Bloom and Stephen part "beneath the lamp of Molly which has been Bloom's guide throughout the day." Litz, "Ithaca," p. 401.

16. Hugh Kenner wittily points out that the scents of "opoponax" and "jessamine" on Molly's drawers are part of Joyce's attempt to create a bourgeois version of *The Odyssey* by giving his Penelope things with Greek and Arabic names that could have been purchased at Sweny the Chemist's in Lincoln Place. Kenner, *The Pound Era* (Berkeley and Los Angeles: University of California Press, 1971), p. 42.

Chapter 9

1. Hugh Kenner has noted that "Penelope" is "the only episode with not one narrative interruption." *Joyce's Voices*, p. 98.

2. Phillip F. Herring has pointed out that Nora's letters to Joyce "are written in a style . . . strikingly similar to Molly's interior monologue." "The Bedsteadfastness of Molly Bloom," *Modern Fiction Studies* 15 (Spring 1969): 49–61, n. 5.

   Surely no other episode contains as many references to letters and the act of writing letters as "Penelope" does. Among them we hear of Bloom's letters during their courtship (615, 634), the letter from Mulvey (624–25), "today's letter" from Boylan and card from Milly (624), and the postcard from Hester Stanhope (621–22), as well as communications to, from, or by such marginal figures as Nancy Blake, a Mrs. Dwenn in Canada, Atty Dillon (624) and Milly's friend Conny Connolly (631).

3. S. L. Goldberg alleges that Molly "can hardly be said to think or to act in her long soliloquy" and that "her stream-of-consciousness is essentially *passive.*" *The Classical Temper,* p. 294.

4. It has been claimed that language supersedes character as Joyce's primary concern in "Penelope." Elaine Unkeless has written: "It is Joyce's languge that makes Molly so alive, but the traits with which he endows her stem from conventional notions of the way a woman acts and thinks." Marilyn French contends that Molly "is built of shreds of realistic but very conventional characteristics of 'women.'" Elaine Unkeless, "The Conventional Molly Bloom," *Women in Joyce,* eds. Suzette Henke and Elaine Unkeless, p. 150; French, *The Book as World,* p. 259.

5. Dorrit Cohn sees "Penelope" as a paradigm of what she calls "autonomous monologue" and the interior monologues of Stephen and Bloom, because of their third-person narrative frames, Cohn sees as examples of "quoted monologue." Dorrit Cohn, *Transparent Minds: Narrative Modes for Presenting Consciousness in Fiction* (Princeton, N.J.: Princeton University Press, 1978), chapters 2 and 6.

6. Expanding upon Gifford and Seidman, Phillip F. Herring devotes an intriguing section in his recent book, *Joyce's Uncertainty Principle,* to the inconsistencies in Molly's Gibraltar memories. Don Gifford and Robert J. Seidman, *Notes for Joyce: An Annotation of James Joyce's "Ulysses,"* p. 509; Phillip F. Herring, *Joyce's Uncertainty Principle* (Princeton, N.J.: Princeton University Press, 1987), pp. 117–40.

7. Of course opoponax, jessamine and the Alameda esplanade are all mentioned in "Penelope" (618, 643, 622, 627).

8. Karen Lawrence argues that "some narrative presence transcribes the sound of the train whistle . . . and, if it performs this act of transcription, it is also scribe for Molly's monologue as well." She concludes: "Even in 'Penelope,' Joyce never totally lets us forget the narrative context of the book." *The Odyssey of Style in "Ulysses,"* p. 204.

9. In the initial style the distance between the narrator and event is never great. David Lodge has observed that when Dlugacz is described as "ferreteyed" and his fingers as "sausagepink" (48) the metaphors are weak "because the two terms of the comparison, the tenor and the vehicle, are not widely separated." Dorrit Cohn also notes that "narrator and character in *Ulysses* not only share the field of vision" but "to some degree the idiom through which they relate it." The same insight forms the basis of Kenner's brilliant chapter on "The Uncle Charles Principle" in *Joyce's Voices.* David Lodge, "The Language of Modernist Fiction: Metaphor and Metonomy," *Modernism,* eds. Malcolm Bradbury, James McFarlane (Harmondsworth: Penguin, 1976), p. 486; Dorrit Cohn, *Transparent Minds,* pp. 71–74; Kenner, *Joyce's Voices,* chapter 2.

10. In an eloquent passage James H. Maddox writes: "Molly unweaves the intricate tapestry of rationality which the two men have woven during the day. In her subversive opposition to the carefully structured and defensive thought-patterns which the two men and the seventeen previous chapters have evolved, Molly is the voice of the unexpected, the unforeseen; she is the voice of potentiality." James H. Maddox, *Joyce's "Ulysses" and the Assault Upon Character,* p. 231.

11. Major Tweedy's military talk has made quite an impression on Bloom; he remembers Rorke's drift once (373) and Plevna several times (46, 394, 583).

12. In his factual dissection of the episode John Henry Raleigh claims that there are two outings with Mulvey, one involving the kiss at the Moorish wall, the other a walk to Europa point and back to O'Hara's tower. Raleigh's *Chronicle* is essential reading for any serious student of 'Penelope." *The Chronicle of Leopold and Molly Bloom: "Ulysses" as Narrative,* p. 62.

13. In her excellent study of parody Linda Hutcheon explores the ways in which it can be affectionate, a kind of detached homage. Hutcheon, *A Theory of Parody: The Teachings of Twentieth-Century Art Forms.*

14.   *Selected Letters of James Joyce,* ed. Richard Ellmann, p. 285.

15.   Dorrit Cohn argues persuasively that Molly's menstruation marks a shift in the monologue from thoughts of the past to thoughts of the future, and that in general these speculations take "the form of scenarios for seducing Stephen and re-seducing Bloom." She concludes: "Her fantasies . . . cluster in the last third of 'Penelope,' whereas memories are denser in the first two-thirds." Cohn, *Transparent Minds,* pp. 219, 228.

16.   In a witty article on *Ulysses* Martin Amis compares the vagaries of the book's prose to the capriciousness of Molly. Amis writes: "The presiding life-force of the book is traditionally thought to be Molly—crooning, yearning, bleeding, squirming, two-timing Molly Bloom. Yet the real superanimator is Joyce's prose, this incredible instrument, half wand, half weapon. In fact, the prose and the heroine have a good deal in common: they are equally fickle, headstrong and vain. One moment she is readied for the tryst, primped and prinked, all lilt and tease, bristling with bedroom know-how and can-do; the next she is immersed in a sour and unfathomable sulk. We know only this: she will have her way." Martin Amis, "The Teacher's Pet," *The Atlantic,* September 1986.

17.   Of course the imitation of Pater, with its reference to the "darker friend" of the Dillon sisters with a brace of cherries "bringing out the foreign warmth" of her skin, constitutes yet another external description of Molly's exotic quality.

Conclusion

1.   Hutcheon, *A Theory of Parody,* pp. 40–43.

2.   Riquelme, *Teller and Tale in Joyce's Fiction,* p. 140.

3.   Ellmann, *James Joyce,* p. 729.

4.   Linda Hutcheon outlines the ways in which literary borrowing or appropriation can be related to plagiarism. *A Theory of Parody,* pp. 39–40.

5.   Lawrence, *The Odyssey of Style in "Ulysses,"* p. 159.

6.   Raleigh, "On the Way Home to Ithaca: the Functions of the 'Eumaeus' Section in *Ulysses*" in Zack Bowen, ed., *Irish Renaissance Annual II,* p. 20.

7.   Interestingly, Joyce did use the word "scorching" with regard to the stylistic progress of his novel. In a letter to Harriet Shaw Weaver he announced that "each successive episode, dealing with some province of artistic culture (rhetoric or music or dialectic), leaves behind it a burnt up field." Ellmann, ed., *Selected Letters of James Joyce,* p. 241.

Bibliography

Joyce Texts

Dubliners. Harmondsworth: Penguin Books, 1976.
Finnegans Wake. London: Faber and Faber, 1939.
The James Joyce Archive. Edited by Michael Groden. New York: Garland Publishing, 1978.
Letters of James Joyce. Vol. 1, edited by Stuart Gilbert. London: Faber and Faber, 1957; Vols. 2 and 3, edited by Richard Ellmann. London: Faber and Faber, 1966.
A Portrait of the Artist as a Young Man. Harmondsworth: Penguin Books, 1960.
Selected Letters of James Joyce. Edited by Richard Ellmann. London: Faber and Faber, 1975.
Stephen Hero. Edited by John J. Slocum and Herbert Cahoon. New York: New Directions, 1944, 1963.
Ulysses: The Corrected Text. Edited by Hans Walter Gabler with Wolfhard Steppe and Claus Melchior. Harmondsworth: Penguin Books, 1986.
Ulysses: A Critical and Synoptic Edition. Edited by Hans Walter Gabler with Wolfhard Steppe and Claus Melchior. New York: Garland Publishing, 1984.
Ulysses: A Facsimile of the Manuscript. Edited by Clive Driver. London: Faber and Faber, 1975.

Secondary Sources

Adams, R. M. "Hades." In Clive Hart and David Hayman, eds., *James Joyce's "Ulysses": Critical Essays*, pp. 91–114. Berkeley: University of California Press, 1974.
Amis, Martin. "The Teacher's Pet." *The Atlantic,* September 1986.
Atherton, J. S. "The Oxen of the Sun." In Clive Hart and David Hayman, eds., *James Joyce's "Ulysses": Critical Essays*, pp. 313–39. Berkeley: University of California Press, 1974.
Baker, Harold D. "Rite of Passage: 'Ithaca,' Style, and the Structures of *Ulysses*" *James Joyce Quarterly* 23, no. 3 (Spring 1986): 277–97.
Bell, Michael. *The Sentiment of Reality: Truth of Feeling in the European Novel.* London: George Allen & Unwin, 1983.
Blackmur, R. P. "The Jew in Search of a Son: Joyce's *Ulysses.*" In *Eleven Essays in the European Novel,* pp. 27–47. New York: Harcourt, Brace & World, 1964.
Bowen, Zack, and James F. Carens, eds. *A Companion to Joyce Studies.* Westport: Conn.: Greenwood Press, 1984.
Bruns, Gerald L. "Eumaeus." In Clive Hart and David Hayman, eds., *James Joyce's "Ulysses": Critical Essays,* pp. 363–83. Berkeley: University of California Press, 1974.
Budgen, Frank. *James Joyce and the Making of "Ulysses."* London: Grayson and Grayson, 1934.
Cohn, Dorrit. *Transparent Minds: Narrative Modes for Presenting Consciousness in Fiction.* Princeton, N.J.: Princeton University Press, 1978.

Copland G. W. Turner. "The Nature of James Joyce's Parody in 'Ithaca.' " *Modern Language Review* 64, no. 4. (October 1969): 759–63.

Cronin, Anthony. *A Question of Modernity.* London: Secker and Warburg, 1966.

Davis, Lennard J. *Resisting Novels: Ideology and Fiction.* London: Methuen, 1987.

Eliot, T. S., ed. *Literary Essays of Ezra Pound.* London: Faber and Faber, 1954.

Ellmann, Richard. *James Joyce.* New York and London: Oxford University Press, 1959.

_____. *Ulysses on the Liffey.* New York: Oxford University Press, 1972.

Fiedler, Leslie. "To Whom Does Joyce Belong? *Ulysses* as Parody, Pop and Porn." In Heyward Ehrlich, ed., *Light Rays: James Joyce and Modernism,* pp. 26–37. New York: New Horizon Press, 1984.

Forster, E. M. *Aspects of the Novel.* London: Edward Arnold, 1927.

French, Marilyn. *The Book as World: James Joyce's "Ulysses."* Cambridge, Mass.: Harvard University Press, 1976.

Gifford Don, and Robert J. Seidman. *Notes for Joyce: An Annotation of James Joyce's "Ulysses."* New York: E. P. Dutton, 1974.

Gilbert, Stuart. *James Joyce's "Ulysses": A Study.* New York: Alfred A. Knopf, 1930; rpt. New York: Vintage Books, 1952.

Glasheen, Adaline. "Calypso." In Clive Hart and David Hayman, eds., *James Joyce's "Ulysses": Critical Essays,* pp. 61–70. Berkeley: University of California Press, 1974.

Goldberg, S. L. *The Classical Temper: A Study of James Joyce's "Ulysses."* London: Chatto and Windus, 1961.

Groden, Michael. *"Ulysses" in Progress.* Princeton, N.J.: Princeton University Press, 1977.

Hanley, Miles L. *Word Index to James Joyce's "Ulysses."* Madison: University of Wisconsin Press, 1937.

Hart, Clive. "Wandering Rocks." In Clive Hart and David Hayman, eds., *James Joyce's "Ulysses": Critical Essays,* pp. 181–216. Berkeley: University of California Press, 1974.

Hayman, David. *"Ulysses": The Mechanics of Meaning.* Englewood Cliffs, N.J.: Prentice-Hall, 1970.

Henke, Suzette. "Gerty MacDowell: Joyce's Sentimental Heroine." In Suzette Henke and Elaine Unkeless, eds., *Women in Joyce,* pp. 132–49. Urbana: University of Illinois Press, 1982.

Herring, Phillip F. "The Bedsteadfastness of Molly Bloom." *Modern Fiction Studies* 15 (Spring 1969): 49–61.

_____. *Joyce's Uncertainty Principle.* Princeton, N.J.: Princeton University Press, 1987.

Hodgart, M. J. C. "Aeolus." In Clive Hart and David Hayman, eds., *James Joyce's "Ulysses": Critical Essays,* pp. 115–30. Berkeley: University of California Press, 1974.

Hutcheon, Linda. *A Theory of Parody: The Teachings of Twentieth-Century Art Forms.* London: Methuen, 1985.

Iser, Wolfgang. *The Implied Reader: Patterns of Communication in Prose Fiction from Bunyan to Beckett.* Baltimore: Johns Hopkins University Press, 1974.

Janusko, Robert. *The Sources and Structures of James Joyce's "Oxen."* Ann Arbor, Mich.: UMI Research Press, 1983.

Jarrell, Mackie L. "Joyce's Use of Swift's *Polite Conversation* in the 'Circe' Episode of *Ulysses.*" *PMLA* 72 (1957): 545–54.

Kellogg, Robert. "Scylla and Charybdis." In Clive Hart and David Hayman, eds., *James Joyce's "Ulysses": Critical Essays,* pp. 147–79. Berkeley: University of California Press, 1974.

Kenner, Hugh. *Dublin's Joyce.* London: Chatto and Windus, 1955.

_____. *Joyce's Voices.* London: Faber and Faber, 1978.

_____. *The Pound Era.* Berkeley and Los Angeles: University of California Press, 1971.

_____. *Ulysses.* London: George Allen & Unwin, 1980.

Kiberd, Declan. *Men and Feminism in Modern Literature.* London: MacMillan, 1985.

Lawrence, Karen. *The Odyssey of Style in "Ulysses."* Princeton, N.J.: Princeton University Press, 1981.

Levin, Harry. *James Joyce.* Norfolk, Conn.: New Directions, 1941.

Littmann, Mark E., and Charles A. Schweighauser. "Astronomical Allusions: Their Meaning and Purpose in *Ulysses.*" *James Joyce Quarterly* 2, no. 4 (summer 1965): 238-46.

Litz, A. Walton. "Ithaca." In Clive Hart and David Hayman, eds., *James Joyce's "Ulysses": Critical Essays,* pp. 385-405. Berkeley University of California Press, 1974.

Lodge, David. "The Language of Modernist Fiction: Metaphor and Metonomy." In Malcolm Bradbury and James MacFarlane, eds., *Modernism,* pp. 481-97. Harmondsworth: Penguin, 1976.

MacCabe, Colin. *James Joyce and the Revolution of the Word.* London: MacMillan, 1978.

McCarthy, Patrick A. "Non-Dramatic Illusion in 'Circe.' " In J. Aubert and M. Jolas, eds., *Joyce and Paris 1902 . . . 1920-1940 . . . 1975: Papers from the Fifth International James Joyce Symposium,* pp. 23-26. Paris: Publications de l'Université de Lille, 1979.

McGee, Patrick. "Joyce's Nausea: Style and Representation in 'Nausicaa.' " *James Joyce Quarterly* 24, no. 3 (spring 1987): 305-18.

Maddox, James H. *Joyce's "Ulysses" and the Assault upon Character.* New Brunswick, N.J.: Rutgers University Press, 1978.

Madtes, Richard. "Joyce and the Building of Ithaca." *Journal of English Literary History* 31 (1964): 443-59.

O'Connor, Frank. *The Lonely Voice: A Study of the Short Story.* Cleveland: The World Publishing Company, 1962.

Orwell, Sonia, and Ian Angus, eds. *The Collected Essays, Journalism and Letters of George Orwell, Volume I: An Age Like This, 1920-1940.* London: Secker and Warburg, 1968.

Parandowski, Jan. "Meeting with Joyce." In Willard Potts, ed., *James Joyce: Portraits of the Artist in Exile,* pp. 154-62. Dublin: Wolfhound Press, 1979.

Peden, William. "A Note or Two on Form and Content in 'Circe.' " In J. Aubert and M. Jolas, eds., *Joyce and Paris 1902 . . . 1920-1940 . . . 1975: Papers from the Fifth International James Joyce Symposium,* pp. 15-16. Paris: Publications de l'Université de Lille, 1979.

Perkins, David. *A History of Modern Poetry.* Cambridge, Mass.: Belknap Press of Harvard University Press, 1976.

Raleigh, John Henry. *The Chronicle of Leopold and Molly Bloom: "Ulysses" as Narrative.* Berkeley: University of California Press, 1977.

————. "On the Way Home to Ithaca: the Functions of the 'Eumaeus' Section in *Ulysses.*" In Zack Bowen, ed., *Irish Renaissance Annual II,* pp. 13-114. London and Toronto: Associated University Presses, 1981.

Read, Forrest, ed. *Pound/Joyce: The Letters of Ezra Pound to James Joyce with Pound's Essays on Joyce.* London: Faber and Faber, 1968.

Riquelme, John Paul. *Teller and Tale in Joyce's Fiction: Oscillating Perspectives.* Baltimore: Johns Hopkins University Press, 1983.

Schneidau, Herbert. "One Eye and Two Levels: On Joyce's 'Cyclops.' " *James Joyce Quarterly* 16, nos. 1/2 (Fall 1978/Winter 1979): 95-103.

Scott, Bonnie Kime. *James Joyce.* Brighton: Harvester Press, 1987.

Senn, Fritz. "Nausicaa." In Clive Hart and David Hayman, eds., *James Joyce's "Ulysses": Critical Essays,* pp. 277-311. Berkeley: University of California Press, 1974.

Shechner, Mark. *Joyce in Nighttown: A Psychoanalytic Inquiry into "Ulysses."* Berkeley: University of California Press, 1974.

Stead, Alistair. "Reflections on Eumaeus: Ways of Error and Glory in 'Ulysses.' " In W. J. McCormack and Alistair Stead, eds., *James Joyce and Modern Literature,* pp. 142-65. London: Routledge and Kegan Paul, 1982.

Thornton, Weldon. *Allusions in "Ulysses": An Annotated List.* Chapel Hill: The University of North Carolina Press, 1968.

Unkeless, Elaine. "The Conventional Molly Bloom." In Suzette Henke and Elaine Unkeless, eds., *Women in Joyce,* pp. 150-68. Urbana: University of Illinois Press, 1982.

Wade, Allan, ed. *The Letters of W. B. Yeats.* London: Rupert Hart-Davis, 1954.

Webb, Eugene. *The Dark Dove: The Sacred and Secular in Modern Literature.* Seattle: University of Washington Press, 1975.

Wilson, Edmund. *Axel's Castle: A Study in the Imaginative Literature of 1870–1930.* New York: Charles Scribner's Sons, 1931; rpt. London: Collins-Fontana, 1961.

Woolf, Virginia. "Modern Fiction." In *Collected Essays, Volume Two,* pp. 103–10. London: Hogarth Press, 1966.

_____. *A Writer's Diary.* London: The Hogarth Press, 1953.

Yeats, W. B. *Essays and Introductions.* London: MacMillan, 1961.

Index